The SUICIDE SOLUTION

The **SUICIDE** SOLUTION

Understanding and Dealing with Suicide from Inside the Mind of Someone Who's Been There

Frank Selden

Archway Publishing books may be ordered through booksellers or by contacting:

Archway Publishing
1663 Liberty Drive
Bloomington, IN 47403
www.archwaypublishing.com
1 (888) 242-5904

Because of the dynamic nature of the Internet, any web addresses or links contained in this book may have changed since publication and may no longer be valid. The views expressed in this work are solely those of the author and do not necessarily reflect the views of the publisher, and the publisher hereby disclaims any responsibility for them.

Any people depicted in stock imagery provided by Thinkstock are models, and such images are being used for illustrative purposes only. Certain stock imagery © Thinkstock.

Scripture quotations taken from the New American Standard Bible®, Copyright © 1960, 1962, 1963, 1968, 1971, 1972, 1973, 1975, 1977, 1995 by The Lockman Foundation. Used by permission. (www.Lockman.org)

ISBN: 978-1-4808-3857-4 (sc)
ISBN: 978-1-4808-3858-1 (hc)
ISBN: 978-1-4808-3859-8 (e)

Library of Congress Control Number: 2016917990

Print information available on the last page.

Archway Publishing rev. date: 12/13/2016

Now I lay me down to sleep
I pray the Lord my soul to take
That I may die before I wake
And safely enter Heaven's Keep

—My nightly prayer for over two years

In memory of T, a good friend I couldn't save,

and

In honor of you who, contemplating death, find
the courage to live the lives you deserve.

Contents

Preface

Recent statistics on suicide report that approximately eighty-six people in the US commit suicide every day. That number includes twenty-two *soldiers,* a term meaning current and former members of all branches of the military. Lowering that statistic requires a change in the way we think and talk about suicide. While I hope this book is part of the changing dialogue, my goal is not primarily to influence national statistics. I want to influence lives—people I care about but cannot reach personally.

You are someone I want to reach. Thank you for reading this book.

If you are buying this book to give to someone, with the hope it might talk him or her out of committing suicide, I want you to reconsider. If you truly want to help, understanding *why* suicide looks attractive to the person will work better than handing over a book you hope will fix things. Please read this book for yourself first; it will help you gain that understanding and provide tools for creating tenable solutions. Then offer to help the person create solutions he or she can believe in. This book is not, by itself, that alternative. It merely points the way. The best thing you can do for your loved one is read it for yourself, and then walk next to him or her. You will know when the time is right to share this book.

If you are reading this book because, like me, you have attempted or contemplated suicide, welcome. All your feelings—especially the dark ones—are accepted here. This book is not an attempt to talk you out of suicide. Suicide is a solution for some, and I am not sitting in judgment of whether or not suicide is the solution for you. My suicide attempts involved frustration with chronic pain, feelings of desperation and guilt, judgment that my life only amounted to failure, and hardwired emotional and cognitive processing that reminded me on a daily basis that I am different from most people.

Do not stop reading after the first section. *If you start this book, please finish it,* and then examine your life again in light of what you learn about yourself. While reading this book—however long it takes—I invite you to respond to thoughts of suicide with "I hear your concern. Let's come up with a different solution for now and revisit suicide after finishing this book."

This book consists of three distinct parts:

- Part 1 addresses the benefits of suicide itself and what suicide solves.
- Part 2 addresses the damage done by suicide.
- Part 3 offers solutions to the problems created by taking one's life.

These topics are addressed from the personal, community, and national perspectives. The term *national* takes into account the ways in which we organize ourselves: political states and nations, religious or ethnic communities, or other ways we identify on group levels.

Some people believe that there are no benefits to suicide. I disagree. Suicidal people see benefits, or they wouldn't consider the option. A group leader at the VA Pain Clinic posed the question, "What benefits do you receive from your pain?" Many of us attending responded that pain has no benefits. The doctor challenged us to examine our lives and be honest with ourselves and each other. One by one, we started to share benefits: an easy out for chores we didn't want to do, time to ourselves when we wanted it, or helping us distinguish what is truly important.

I firmly believe that suicide, like pain, can benefit us individually, as a family or community, and as a state or nation. An honest discussion of suicide needs to include seeing the benefits. Otherwise we will not be able to communicate with those contemplating suicide. Trust me, when I made plans to end my life, I focused on the benefits. If someone wanted to talk me out of finalizing a suicide plan but was not willing to engage in an honest discussion of benefits as I saw them—making blanket statements such as *There is nothing to gain*—the conversation ended immediately.

Some of the benefits may be hard to accept. We may need to face realities about ourselves, personal communities, and public societies we want to ignore or gloss over or characterize as something more acceptable.

It was not enough for me to make a commitment not to end my life. I made such a commitment after one attempt, but, in the emotional distress leading up to the next, the commitment meant nothing to me other than one more expectation I would fail to fulfill. Now, I want to give people a reason to live.

The world needs you more than ever. I need you. That may be hard to accept, given that I don't even know you. But I hope you will understand my meaning by the end of the book.

—*Frank Selden*
Seattle, August, 2016

PART 1

SUICIDE'S
BENEFITS

CHAPTER 1
PERSONAL BENEFITS

Thus, I am left with basically nothing. Too trapped in a war to be at peace, too damaged to be at war. Abandoned by those who would take the easy route, and a liability to those who stick it out—and thus deserve better. So you see, not only am I better off dead, but the world is better without me in it

This is what brought me to my actual final mission. Not suicide, but a mercy killing. I know how to kill, and I know how to do it so that there is no pain whatsoever. It was quick, and I did not suffer. And above all, now I am free. I feel no more pain. I have no more nightmares or flashbacks or hallucinations. I am no longer constantly depressed or afraid or worried

I am free.[1]

—Portion of a suicide note by soldier Daniel Somers

1

Let's begin by looking inside the thoughts of those who believe that suicide is the best solution to all their problems.

If you've never been suicidal, it's difficult to imagine how suicide can seem a viable and ethical solution. Perhaps you judge suicidals[2] as selfish, simply not seeing things clearly, or out of their minds. This is a disservice to those who are in such a desperate situation. In my case, I saw things clearly. I was not out of my mind, and I immediately dismissed anyone who approached me that way.

I want to give you a glimpse of what it feels like on the inside for someone who sees his physical, emotional, and spiritual pain as utterly untenable.

If you have been—or are—suicidal, some of my reasoning and thoughts may seem familiar to you.

- "It's my decision."
- "Suicide will end the physical and emotional pain I'm in."
- "Suicide is the only permanent solution."

It's My Decision

History contains few stories of people who leave this planet alive. Death comes for all: the just and the unjust, slave and free-born, and the wealthy (safely ensconced in protective walls) and homeless beggars sleeping on cardboard beds under a freeway on-ramp. We often pretend that resisting death is the ultimate duty or goal of the living. Is this a duty we owe to God, each other, or ourselves? I reject all three choices.[3] My duty regarding death, if one exists at all, is the same as my duty regarding life: live and die with intention. I intend to die. For me, why is obvious; it is an end to my emotional, physical, social, and spiritual suffering. My most important question is how to achieve this end.

Deliberately ending my life is the ultimate personal freedom. No matter what any person or government takes from me, this one freedom remains. Society can tie me to a gurney with thick straps, isolate me in a room containing nothing with which to hurt myself, or keep me under constant surveillance. Yet, like a prisoner of war in an enemy camp, I will find a way to break free. It is my mission and my duty to escape their bonds. If I die as I intend, perhaps the book of my life will end with its only success. Many want to deny me my ultimate triumph; they tell me I must continue living, if not for my own purpose then for theirs.

But constantly dealing with emotional, physical, and spiritual pain is not living. Some animals, when one leg is caught in a trap, will gnaw that leg off to free themselves rather than slowly bleed to death. How do I set myself free when my entire being is ensnared? Some people quote Psalm 91:3 to me, stating that it is God who will deliver me from the snare of the trapper. My experience, however, feels like my God has forsaken me.

Ending the Physical Pain

I can no longer relate to others. I sip a sugar-free vanilla latte alone in a crowded coffee house, contemplating recent changes in my life. I have constant pain—pain that redefines my personal level 10. Friends attempt to comfort me with well-intentioned but meaningless phrases such as "At least you came home in one piece." Stupid. If I came home without a foot, I would still be in one piece, just not the same size piece that deployed. A missing foot stops hurting. Lucky me, I guess, that my being in one piece just produces pain on a constant basis. Aggravating pain. Draining pain. Debilitating pain.

My inner radar, constantly surveying surroundings, people, and conversations, fixates on a nearby conversation.

"Paper cuts are the worst!" A lady sucks a drop of blood from the tip of her right index finger. "I think it's because the cut is so fine. They really hurt!"

A paper cut? Your 10—your worst pain—is *a paper cut?* No one understands! Walking hurts, bending hurts, sleeping hurts, holding my grandkids hurts. Running is impossible. My life is completely upended because of pain, and she complains about a paper cut she'll forget about in three days. My judgments further detach me from those around me.

No one understands. People tell me they don't want to hear me describing my pain in response to questions about my return to civilian life. My life permanently changes, and I can't talk about it? I look the same but I'm not, and no one gets it, outside of the few who know from personal experience such as vets in the VA pain clinic. Physical activities that once brought joy now burden me with pain. Happiness eludes me. Gratitude seems blasphemous. My anger alienates people. I do not blame them, but I feel abandoned. I do not want this life of constant pain as my experience. My freedom, my hope, is in letting go.

There's no fix. Doctors tell me that surgery for this pain is too risky. Where I was wounded in the spine is both the most painful and most difficult to fix. They recommend physical therapy and drugs. In week one of physical therapy I learn how to walk to avoid exacerbating my injury and increasing pain levels. I feel like I'm a two-year-old again, dependent on others in nearly every aspect of my existence, and I hate it.

Pills reduce pain, relax muscles, and reduce swelling, but for me, it means dealing with level-10 pain in a disengaged stupor rather than screaming agony. People tell me they enjoy massages. They bring some relief, as does lying flat on my back with my knees elevated. Yet within moments after a massage ends rising from the mat, muscles begin to spasm, nerves twitch, and pain elevates. Every waking moment of every day I want this pain to end, but there is no end in sight.

I just want it to end. Physical life is designed to be enjoyed! I found bliss in walking barefoot through new grass and warm sand, snorkeling and mountain climbing, and company runs and obstacle courses. There was pleasure in travel and socializing with friends and having sex. Now— nothing. Sometimes I prefer the stupor of strong drink to the numbing effect of pills. Taken together, I end up in a painful contortion on the floor, throwing up on myself. Tried it.

One IED blast, two minutes of my life replayed repeatedly in slow motion in my mind, and my life morphed from enjoyment to agony.

How much pain do I need to endure in life before life is not worth enduring? Who gets to judge? In the midst of her pain, paper-cut lady didn't talk about suicide. (Yes, I might judge her if she did, just as I judged her for her comment.) I wonder, though, if she knew about my pain, would she judge me if I wanted to end it by ending my life?

Permanently ending my pain appeals to me more than spending months to years in therapy and using drugs. Some will understand; others may judge me as selfish or weak. One trigger squeeze and it's all over. Not even their opinions matter anymore.

Ending the Emotional Pain

When people tell me I can choose to be happy, I want to shove a positive-thinking book down their throats and see what happy choices they make. Emotional pain unravels the fabric of my life; it shatters identity, alters reality, and subverts relationships. In some emotional states people can no more choose happiness than they can choose to become Chinese, female, or a Leo.

I did my best to make positive thoughts fix my world as a kid, but they didn't. I hoped positive thinking would erase the emotional pain of judging myself to be different from other kids, of living in poverty that resulted in hand-me-down clothes or having to work from the age of ten to help support my family. I watched the Disney film *Pollyanna* several times, believing that thinking good about my world would help create happiness. I played the "Glad Game" by myself, imagining Pollyanna was with me. I believed so strongly in my ability to play the game that, at the age of twelve, I felt invincible.

Positive thinking and counting my blessings did not eviscerate my anguish. By internalizing the message that I could control my emotional state by choosing to do so, it set up an internal war between hope and despair, and I judged myself somehow broken for not being able to think my way out of my pain. I became convinced that if I died and a coroner performed an autopsy, the coroner would find something wrong with my brain. "Oh, this explains everything!" my make-believe coroner would announce, verifying that indeed I was different from everyone else and would never truly belong.

In my twenties, when I became a single dad to three young children the summer before my senior year of ministerial school, I stopped playing the Glad Game. I stopped believing that thinking better about people or circumstances or myself would make a difference. Divorce not only ended what I thought was the only marriage I could have in this lifetime, it also ended a career I felt called to join. My denomination did not accept divorcees as ministers. No amount of positive thinking could restore my family or my career hopes. I fell into a despair that lasted more than ten years, believing myself a complete failure.

In my early thirties I decided to restore my life by going back to school and signing up for the Army National Guard. I loved both, and my energy for life returned. A few years later, I remarried. An undergraduate degree turned into law school, and weekend warrior training with the Army National Guard resulted in two tours in Iraq.

War changed everything. Reality shattered the lens through which I viewed the world. The world became less safe and people less trustworthy. Random acts of violence reminded me how little control I wielded over my future. I came to consider that a government I once believed in, and for which I volunteered to defend with my life, lied. It wasn't just about weapons of mass destruction, but, more importantly, it was about bringing freedom to the Iraqi people. We were forcing political solutions on their country once again, just as we did after World War I. Iraqis wanted us out of their country. The war was not about Iraq; it was about the United States and protecting its interests. We used Iraq and the Iraqi people for our own selfish purposes, and they knew it.

I felt lied to about the exceptionality of American democracy. I felt lied to about the military's role in defending our freedom. Where I once gave speeches supporting our military, I now looked at recruiting as nothing more than Honest John luring children to Pleasure Island in Disney's *Pinocchio*, producing monsters to serve at the whim of an-all-too-real Coachman for political power and monetary profit.

Despair returned. My wife, who I adored, understandably did not want to be married to the person I became after my tours. My emotional state also affected my new career. I dropped back into a dark, chaotic place, this time with anger, resentment, shame, and loathing. I became a recluse and was convinced that if it took me ten years to rebound last time, this time I would likely never recover. Living no longer interested me.

Some people believe hatred is the worst emotional state. I disagree. At least hatred gives people a reason to live. For me, the foulest emotional state is limitless chaos beyond my control.

While the basis for our emotional states can take (as mine did) a lifetime to develop, there are times when a precipitating event, especially a loss that seems uncontrollable, can push us to the point where a permanent solution seems to be the only way out. That's the way it was for the following suicidals.

The loss of a child. She needed a few things from the grocery store, so she fastened her seat belt, checked her mirrors, looked over her right shoulder, and backed out of her driveway. They were routine behaviors, performed hundreds of times. Then came a thud, a scream, and silence. Horror gripped her as she exited the car faster than humanly possible. Her youngest child, only two, lay dead under the vehicle. Another scream, this time the emotional pain of a mother shrieking in an agony no one else could possibly understand. How did her baby get outside without anyone noticing? Why didn't the other kids watch her? Why did God let this happen? Time did not heal the wounds. Although no one blamed her, she blamed herself. Her family once filled her life with joy; now, looking into their eyes, she saw tragedy. She also blamed God. An omnipotent God could have prevented this! Church, once a source of solace, could not ease her pain. There was no balm in Gilead capable of drying her tears.

The loss of family. He returned home from a week-long conference. As he pulled into the driveway, something seemed different. No lights were on in the house. He walked into the kitchen from the garage.

"Honey? Jason? Julie?" There was no response from a woman he adored or the two most wonderful children in the world. Seeing a note on the counter, he smiled, grateful for his considerate bride. It would explain when they would be home. Except the note said they were not coming home. She had moved away and would not tell him where; she said a lawyer would be contacting him. He raced through the house in disbelief. In their bedroom all her clothes were gone. The kids' rooms were empty, and even the furniture wasn't there. How? Why? Eventually he would discover his wife's affair, his family living in a different man's home, a clandestine move planned for months, and all of it a huge surprise. How could he not have known? How could love be this blind? He would never trust love again. His entire life had been betrayed by the one person who could hurt him the most. He always looked forward to coming home from business trips. Now everything seemed meaningless. An infinite number of people offered to join him for company, but they could not cure his loneliness. Books recommended by friends only accentuated his sorrow. His mental pictures about people, the world, and himself blew up into a million tiny jigsaw puzzle pieces, and he did not even want to put them back together.

The loss of honor. It's an interesting phrase: *No boots on the ground.* He wore boots, and, as a forward observer, he was definitely on the ground. Intelligence intercepted cell calls about a *wedding,* a code word for a gathering of Islamic terrorist cell leaders with someone from higher up in the organization. He communicated on a scrambled SAT phone the arrival of the first "guests" to the location. There were about twenty males, busy with preparations, and one seemed to watch the only road from the south. A few men disappeared into the only house in the area, a location not previously known as a cell location, which strengthened the rationale indicating a high-level meeting. Planes were en route with precision missiles; his job was now to set a laser beam the guidance systems would follow to this exact location. Fifteen minutes later, a few of the men start gesturing. Three vehicles approached, all black Mercedes. He called in the hit: "target arriving."

On this mission the target was not anyone in particular. Back in the US, the president's low approval numbers meant launching another mission that would come across as tough leadership in the news. Directives "from the highest level" set up a mission where we would strike first and sort out the bodies later. If we killed a high-level target, so much the better, but that was not as important as a successful air strike announced by the president on international television. He hated politics and was glad to be as far away from DC as possible.

He focused his long-range binoculars on a man smiling as he reached for the back door of the third Mercedes. The door opened. A gloved hand reached out, and a white dress emerged. The bride's smile turned to horror as the missile hits precisely on target and on time. Over thirty innocent locals were killed. Intel had gotten it wrong. It was a real wedding. These were innocent people, not "acceptable loses." He would be told he was only doing his job, but acting as a pawn in situations where "national security" often meant protecting a politician's career was not why he enlisted. This time he could not shrug off his guilt. The expression on her face as she looked up toward a noise she didn't understand, followed by an explosion she didn't deserve, branded this tragedy into the mind of the only person in the world who knew the truth but who was prohibited (under penalty of a dishonorable discharge) from ever revealing it. Guilt and hatred work insidious magic when they claim a man's soul.

The loss of dreams. A baby would solve everything! He would soon leave for college; one she had applied to but from which she had received a rejection letter. Her parents supported her attending any of three colleges that offered her admission. They did not even want to discuss her moving to *his* college town, looking for work, and reapplying. However, she wanted *him*. If she became pregnant, he would want to marry her. Her parents would then accept her moving in with him, and her idealized life could begin. So she stopped taking her pills. When she shared her wonderful test results with him, his reaction stunned her. He disowned her, called her irresponsible and manipulative, and said he never wanted to see her again. Her mother kept repeating statistics about the plight of unwed mothers. Her father wondered how his princess had turned into a whore. Friends laughed at her. Everywhere she turned life shamed her. This was not a world into which she wanted to bring a child. A visit to a clinic terminated the life of her baby, but this action did not restore her life to her. Nothing could.

Blame, regret, betrayal, guilt, hatred, shame; these are powerful emotions that can tear a soul into pieces that will never reassemble. One common element to all this emotional pain is their solution: suicide. Some wounds do not heal. People try counselling, prayer, drugs, moving to a new city, reading recommended books, isolation, alcohol, or staying busy, but, when the memories still return just because they hear a baby cry, or see a face that reminds them, they want the pain to end. Permanently.

A Permanent Way Out

A new mental health (MH) worker at the VA asked me, "Do you have a plan?"

"I have six plans," I replied in a matter of fact tone.

She paused, as if not knowing how to process my answer.

"Six plans? That you can implement today?"

"Yes."

My nonplussed manner did not help her determine if I presented a current threat to myself and thus warranted involuntary intervention. The existence of a plan, the means to carry out that plan, and a time line indicates a high risk and may warrant immediate action to protect suicidals from themselves.

"Are you saying you are planning to hurt yourself?"

No, I explained, I have no current desire to harm myself. However, just like DOD develops plans that might activate, depending on conditions, I also have several plans to terminate my life. Plans designed to succeed. Plans I can implement any time I decide.

"Are you safe?"

"Yes, I am safe," I replied, nodding my head.

She needed to hear this to move on. More accurately, I needed her to hear it, as I did not want to move into the next phase of interacting with MH if she perceived I posed a danger to myself or others. In the Seattle VA community, we refer to this as "avoiding the seventh floor", the confinement ward.

People who say suicide isn't an option are as delusional as people who say failure is not an option. Not only is suicide an option but it is one option which, if successful, provides a permanent solution to the issues that give rise to the contemplation of options. However, as a society, we are unwilling to acknowledge this fact, and it leads to further alienation of those who are suicidal.

My MH worker knew too well that suicide was an option. In my case, six options. What most people really mean by "not an option" is that they do not create a plan for options they aren't willing to implement. Refusing to acknowledge suicide as an option is a denial of reality, an irresponsible attitude perpetuated by people willing to acknowledge only those solutions they deem appropriate and that they would implement.

Some people judge suicide as the ultimate selfish expression.[4] I find that to be a grotesquely selfish attitude, placing other's needs over those of the person contemplating suicide.

Others minimize suicide as a permanent solution to a temporary problem. Tell that to Robin Williams or thousands of other people who continue to struggle with permanent issues that, because they are not visible, our culture tends to minimize.

As a society, we pathologize thoughts of willingly ending one's life to the point where we will physically stop the attempt. From the suicide's point of view, forced compliance seems selfish and cruel.

If I want to end my life, why should I be compelled to continue my existence for someone else's benefit? You judge me as mentally unstable because, in your judgment, a mentally stable person would not want to end his or her life. Then you force me into a confined existence, treat me like a caged animal, and then have the audacity to pride yourself on your humanitarian efforts. Years later I die, because all humans do. So what did you accomplish other than forcibly exerting your will onto my life to delay the inevitable? Your treatment of human beings, your view of yourself, the policies you create, and the force you employ are the selfish acts. In fact, you are part of the problem of why some people do not want to live in this world you created. You like your solution. I like mine. Suicide is my safety blanket, my emergency contingency plan for resolving a maelstrom from which it seems there is no other escape.

I have dealt with these issues my entire life. Take drugs to help me get through what you see as temporary? Numb my mind so I don't see reality anymore? Allow you to control my life, with me as the marionette and you the mastermind? No thank you. I reject your arrogant God complex, your misleading clichés. You don't listen. Furthermore, you believe you don't have to listen because you already know what is right for me. You do not understand the problem if you view it as temporary. You are right about the permanence of the solution. About that we can agree. The choice to end my own life on my terms is one of the greatest expressions of my personal liberty, one of the few liberties that no one can take away.

Is suicide the best option for everyone in every precarious situation? No. However, I do believe that suicide is an appropriate option for some people in some circumstances. Who gets to make this decision? Individuals. When, as a community and nation, we can acknowledge that suicide is a legitimate option and solution and when we stop minimizing the issues or dismissing terrible thoughts and feelings, then suicidals will turn to us for help. Until then, we're part of the problem that their suicides solve for them.

CHAPTER 2

COMMUNITY BENEFITS

Thank you all from the pit of my burning, nauseous stomach for your letters and concern during the past years. I'm too much of an erratic, moody baby! I don't have the passion anymore, and so remember, it's better to burn out than to fade away.

Peace, love, empathy.

Kurt Cobain

Frances and Courtney, I'll be at your alter.

Please keep going Courtney, for Frances.

For her life, which will be so much happier without me.

I LOVE YOU, I LOVE YOU![5]

I answered the phone with my usual "This is Frank."

"Frank Selden?"

"Yes."

"You don't know me, but I am T's brother." Right for the second time. I did not know him, but I knew about him.

T was an attorney friend of mine who moved away from his east coast family. He considered me one of his few real friends. While he probably shared more about his life with me than anyone in the Seattle area, it still did not amount to much. I knew he had no desire to return home. A few weeks before this call, T cleanly ended his life with a bullet from his concealed weapon revolver. His brother wanted to know whether I knew why. Was there a note or anything that could explain this tragedy? I wondered whether the brother actually cared or did his questioning hint at a family scandal he wished would not become public.

I find it interesting that many people try to look for one reason, as if the straw that broke the camel's back was more important than the rest of the pile. I am convinced that T's pile included numerous family issues, yet I reassured this brother that T expressed a lack of hope for the future, not remorse or regret for the past. He sounded relieved and thanked me for my time. I judged that T's family slept better that night. One properly placed bullet and family secrets remained hidden.

A young woman, "V," shared her reason for contemplating suicide: her family would be better off without her. I asked if she asked talked to them about this assessment, or was it a thought she told herself was true. One of her family members spoke these irresponsible words on more than one occasion and said that everyone in the family felt the same way. V believed that person. I did not.

"Have you asked others if they feel this way?"

"No."

I occasionally volunteer to help people who are contemplating suicide. V came to me as a referral from someone who knew my story and thought I could help. Like Abraham Lincoln, I find that my own wisdom, coupled with the wisdom of everyone around me, seems insufficient for my task. I often rely on divine intuition to guide me to the real problems and causes. With V, I found myself instantly seeking wisdom. If I recommended that she ask others in her family, what they said did not matter as much as what V heard or believed. Based on her mental state, one negative comment about lack of acceptance could push her over the edge. I did not know her family and did not trust them to constructively handle this issue. Confronting her family also could force V to admit she was contemplating suicide, a recommendation to which she strenuously objected.

V's suicidal thoughts focused on solving community problems, although they were based on someone else's statements rather than her own conclusions. Either way, with a few pills her problems would be solved.

Whether community problems are indeed solved with someone's suicide depends on several factors, including what people believe about suicide. Today we find it hard to believe that someone throwing herself into a volcano actually appeased volcano gods, so they wouldn't rain molten lava on the village. Yet if everyone in V's family believed they would be better off if she took her own life, they would convince themselves of that result, just as the village shaman reminded everyone that the village did not perish because of the sacrifices.

Too often a counselor can convince family members to stop saying certain phrases. That does not, however, change the dynamic. Human dynamics are more complex than the mere words someone utters. We can discern (or believe we discern) attitudes, judgments, opinions, and emotions from body language: eye movements, facial expressions, and gestures. To change V's mind about what her family believed would require a change of heart—not an omission of words—from everyone in her family. Humans instinctively comprehend the truth that

> He that complies against his will
> Is of his own opinion still
> Which he may adhere to, yet disown,
> For reasons to himself best known.[6]

This applies to V, as well as her family. I could convince her, for a moment, not to kill herself. We could discuss safety plans, create emergency contacts, and make her promise to call someone first. However, unless she changes her mind about what she believes, she will remain pulled by the collective consciousness of her community toward suicide as the solution to their imbroglio.

In April 2014, TIME published "9 Musicians Remember Kurt Cobain."[7] These musicians, who were part of Kurt's community, recognized that the spirit through which Cobain connected to millions in a misfit generation also drove him to suicide. Cobain believed he lost his passion. He seemed to believe that a musician who loses his passion will fade away into a life Kurt evidently did not want for himself. He also believed the daughter he loved more than his own life would be better off without him. Given their Child Protective Services issues at the time, one can understand his conclusions. Given the subsequent history between Courtney and Frances, I am not sure that their lives became happier without him.

M's husband passed away several years before I met her. She confided that she knew her children conspired to place her in a nursing home, sell her house, spend all her money, and never visit her. She wanted me to help her make sure that didn't happen. She dreaded losing control of her senses and did not want to be the sort of burden to her family that she witnessed in several situations close to her. In the state of Washington physicians are only allowed to not connect someone to or disconnect someone from artificially induced hydration and nutrition if that individual is declared terminal. M wanted to die before terminal conditions set in. Some people thought she had already passed that threshold, but I did not. Still, I was not about to engage in an activity that state laws defined as murder.

I asked whether or not she had discussed with her three children how they would care for her if necessary. She did not trust her two sons. She trusted her daughter, but despite her daughter's willingness to care for her mother in her own home as long as necessary, M knew such care would place a burden on her daughter—a single mother to a teenaged daughter of her own.

By taking a few pills she already possessed, the community issues would vanish. Her children could fight over the inheritance. She did not care about the money, only that she didn't become a burden to her daughter and no one would place her in a home.

Who gets to decide whether or not suicide presents a potential solution for community problems? Only one person: the one contemplating the action. Everyone else may provide input, but this is not a group vote. I prefer individuals contemplating suicide to discuss impacts and consequences rather than make assumptions about what other people believe or feel. Still, I know too well that such discussions can give others an opportunity to initiate involuntary confinement proceedings or other restrictive measures the individual does not want. Honesty is not always the best policy.

The End of Community Pain

For more than ten years I wished someone a painful death for all the agony she caused me. I would not do anything to ensure her untimely demise because, if anything mysterious happened, I would be suspect number one. The thought, *why don't you just kill yourself?* crossed my mind hundreds of times, although I never said it to her. This was my pain, not hers, and I imagine that ending her life never crossed her mind. Today we cross paths, engage in civil discourse, and I honestly wish her happiness whenever I think of her. Community pain does not always last forever. In some social settings, though, the turmoil never ends.

Suicide can solve some community problems, if only in the minds of those contemplating such a solution. Right now, there's a suicidal in the communal circle of someone reading this book. Conceding that his or her suicide could resolve community pain may feel like giving permission or giving impetus to the journey you don't want the person to take. But denying this potential increases the turbulence. Why? Perhaps it's because you refuse to listen.

Set aside judgments for a minute, and hear the person out. Listen carefully to the words and absorb their meaning. You do not have to agree. Can you at least see why, in his or her mind, suicide appeals as a solution to problems? Try saying these words: "I can see why suicide appeals to you as a solution to X."

Now it's your turn. What alternatives do you offer? If your reply begins with "You can't" or "You shouldn't," don't bother engaging. Come up with a better solution first. Perhaps you don't have a solution, but your truth is "I don't want you to!" Say that. Platitudes and moral imperatives only push suicidals deeper into their resolutions to die. If you don't have a solution but are willing to be part of one, let them know what you are willing to do.

Addressing community pain is not about creating a safety contract; it is about getting to the heart of why suicide entices people as a solution to community pain. What is the root of the pain? Solve that if you want to help. Your suicidal already has a solution in mind.

CHAPTER 3

NATIONAL BENEFITS

By fulfilling its objective to alleviate human suffering, medicine is however continually bound to respecting the self-determination of human beings. No one is allowed to treat a patient against his or her will. That doctors are only permitted to introduce or terminate medical procedures with the express permission of the patient is now a generally accepted fact. For example, whether or not a life-prolonging procedure is introduced or terminated is always and exclusively dependent on the agreement of the patient involved.

When medical ethics, as described above, are based on the alleviation of suffering and the respect of self-determination, it should be obvious that these ethics are completely compatible with assisted suicide, since a doctor who fulfils the request of a terminally-ill patient to stop all further therapy and prescribe a lethal medication is alleviating suffering and respecting self-determination.[8]

I have no idea if anyone at the Unites States national level surveys issues across our country and concludes an increase in suicide rates, perhaps among certain populations, would alleviate fiscal pressures or make our government's job of governing easier. Although I find many federal and state government programs intrusively manipulative for a free society, I am not enough of a believer in conspiracy theories to conclude any level of government secret agendas to encourage select groups of people to off themselves.

Linda Thompson, an Indianapolis lawyer, quit her year-old general practice in 1993 to run the American Justice Federation, a for-profit group that promotes pro-gun causes and various conspiracy theories. She published a list called "The Clinton Body Count: Coincidence or the Kiss of Death?" that contained the names of thirty-four people with ties to the Clinton family who she believed died suspiciously.[9] The Clinton body count conspiracy resurfaced in 2016 with the mysterious murder of Seth Rich.[10]

I became aware of Thompson's list in 1994 when Representative William Dannemeyer (R-CA) published a letter to congressional leaders listing twenty-four people with some connection to Clinton who had died "under other than natural circumstances" and called for hearings on the matter. Of this list, Vince Foster's suicide seemed the most potentially credible cover-up to me. I wondered whether presidents have access to invisible groups who can murder people when it's convenient to "national security" and plant enough evidence to make an independent inquiry rule the death a suicide. I now believe that our government is not in the business of murdering citizens in suicidal fashion to resolve national tribulations or presidential personal problems.

This section is not about decisions to manufacture murders as suicides or policies to promote suicides for political gain. It is simply asking whether or not suicide, as a national phenomenon, solves any public issues, and, if so, is there anything we can learn from this knowledge about addressing suicide? For this quest I turn to the one federal agency I know anything about, the Department of Defense (DOD).

Suicide by active duty military personnel and veterans continues to foster national attention.[11] Coupled with reports of veterans dying while waiting for services, some falsely reported as rendered, this attention tarnishes the reputation of a department once held in the highest esteem. I do not know of any veterans who decided to end their lives solely to benefit their nation. Rather, some intended to make a statement such as "See how f-in' stupid this is? I can't take this anymore!"

DOD blames these suicides on mental health issues rather than policies. Perhaps rightly so, yet I noticed that, rather than taking the initiative, DOD stepped up efforts to counter suicide after public pressure, based on unacceptable numbers, forced it to. Did DOD not consider suicide an issue? Did policy makers see benefits in allowing the trend to continue?

I can think of a few benefits: a self-weeding of undesirable psychological profiles, financial savings from not paying a lifetime of monetary or health benefits, and shorter wait times at medical or mental health facilities. No, I do not believe that anyone in DC, DOD, or any other agency ever consciously made a decision to support policies that increased suicides in order to gain these or other benefits.

We now, thankfully, see policies shifting to create these benefits in ways other than relying on continued increases in suicides. Psychological profiles can help recruiting efforts reject individuals with certain characteristics. With congressionally approved active duty military numbers being lower recruiting efforts can focus on people who will do well not only in combat but in their personal lives. Shifting focus to prevention, while more labor intensive, saves money in the long run in terms of medical and mental health costs and allows more care for more people. Allowing some veterans to seek care outside the military or VA systems is shortening lines.

These results from the public pressure about suicide numbers will not make much difference to suicidals. They ended their lives for personal or community reasons. This is not a Gandhi-style hunger strike in which, after the demands are met, people return to eating a healthy diet. People are suffering. Some choose to end their suffering by ending their lives.

In the US suicide is frequently violent. We leave people little choice. Our government bans the retail sale of less violent alternatives. In the past, this is what we asked them to do through our representative government. While we work on easing the suffering that leads people to commit suicide, I suggest we also work to alleviate the suffering people experience in suicide.

Under Washington state law, and in most states, if I have an incurable and irreversible condition certified to be terminal, where the application of life-sustaining treatment would serve only to artificially prolong the process of my dying, I am allowed to direct in advance that such treatment be withheld or withdrawn and that I be permitted to die naturally. We exercise this advance consent through the use of a written instrument commonly called a *Living Will*, signed in a state of proper mental capacity and properly witnessed. This concept is, correctly, not considered suicide.

Washington is currently one of three states that allows physician-assisted suicide. When a terminally ill person follows specific protocols, physicians are allowed to write a prescription for medication the client ingests on his or her own. The term *terminal disease* means "an incurable and irreversible disease that has been medically confirmed and will, within reasonable medical judgment, produce death within six months."[12] Does the state benefit from these laws? Perhaps, through reduced long-term medical care costs or Medicare payments. The citizens of Washington did not pass this legislation to financially benefit the state. We passed this bill—and, yes, I voted in favor—to create a safe environment for people to exercise their decisions to end their lives on their own terms.

This legislation, however, does not apply to most military-related suicides. A study released by the Pentagon in 2013 showed that military suicides are related not to combat, as previous studies suggested, but to alcohol and depression.[13] My inner skeptic believes this Pentagon-backed study is an attempt to divert blame to something it doesn't control. Even if the study found an objective way to distinguish between a mental health diagnosis and combat as independent factors, I still would not believe this study. Training people to kill others on command and obey orders without hesitation plays with the human psyche. We destroy,[14] in the name of honor, liberty, freedom, and justice. Yet the purpose of many missions relates more to political manipulations than these values. I strongly believe that the way our military recruits, trains, and deploys troops helps create the mental issues that lead to military suicide. The root cause is not mental illness itself.

In our civilian communities, the mental stresses that can lead to suicide (or murder) increase proportionately to population densities, crime, safety, health, and many other factors. Not yet appearing in national headlines is a factor I expect our government to ignore even more than it ignores how military policy creates suicidal conditions. This factor is the increasing bureaucratic intrusion into and administrative control over the lives of people with a cultural history of personal liberty. If suicide rates increase, we may shrug our shoulders and say, "That's okay, they didn't fit in." Thus we accept, or at least attain, another national advantage.

National benefits from suicide include decreased medical and mental health costs, decreased demands on our medical and mental health treatment systems, and a perception that our society is less stressful overall. But recognizing and realizing benefits is only part of the story. These benefits might not be worth the cost.

PART 2

SUICIDE'S
HARM

CHAPTER 1
PERSONAL HARM

I awoke from the coma two and a half days later. I should have died from drug overdose as a result of taking all those pills, a mistake for which payment was due immediately. I had foot drop and nerve damage in both feet. When I awoke from my coma was my right foot was twisted from the drugs I had taken in my suicide attempt. I hobbled out of bed realizing that my suicide attempt was a mistake because I was actually glad to be still alive. The treatment following my near-fatal suicide attempt consisted of rehab for foot drop over the next three months. I was homeless for eight months after my release from the hospital. I should not have ignored my depression by not seeking treatment which was my responsibility.[15]

When someone asks me to talk to a family member or friend dealing with potential suicide, the person often hopes I can convince the loved one not to follow through with such a plan. Before accepting such invitations, I let people know I do not convince anyone. I am happy to share my story and insights and help them develop their own reasons. Hearing "I want you to convince my friend not to commit suicide" is as repugnant to me as someone walking into my law office, asking, "I want you to create a will for my mom, leaving everything to me."

If I create a will for Mom, Mom gets to decide the terms. I do not allow anyone else present, other than the client, to mention terms. I give them one warning, but if they continue to say things such as "Mom, remember … you said you wanted me to have …" out they go. Sometimes people believe they are constrained by moral or social law to include certain provisions in their wills. We discuss the freedom our society allows; that means they may make those decisions, unencumbered by fraud, duress, or undue influence. We discuss the fact that they are not required to leave property to anyone, including their children. We focus our discussion on the question, "What do you want to do?" Sometimes I help people see that external factors shaped what they initially thought they wanted to do. By removing those limitations, they understand what they truly want. Anyone can create a will on the Internet for a fraction of what I charge. The value I add is counsel, feedback, permission, and drawing out of them what is right for them.

Deciding terms for ending one's life is even more important than terms for distributing property at the end of one's life. Yet there are those who want to interfere in this decision and add undue influence through "rules" that don't exist. Let's dismiss two of these.

Do Suicides Go Straight to Hell?

Thomas Aquinas, a philosopher, theologian, and Angelicus Doctor of the Catholic Church, who died in1274, believed that confession of sin must be made prior to departure from this world to the next. He taught that suicide was the most fatal of all sins because the victim could not repent of it. Although that teaching is no longer church doctrine,[16] I find that many people today who believe in hell also believe that people who commit suicide are doomed to that eternity. One of my teachers at the Loma Linda School of Religion taught that any unforgiven sin at the end of one's life meant time in hell. He also taught hell as a temporary, not eternal state, so perhaps going to hell for any sin, including suicide, isn't as bad as some describe.

In Dante's *Inferno*, suicides are in the center ring of the seventh circle. The outer ring houses murderers and those who were violent to other people and property. There, Dante sees Dionysius I of Syracuse, Guy de Montfort, and the Centaurus sinking into a river of boiling blood and fire. In the middle ring, the poet sees suicides turned into trees and bushes, which are fed upon by harpies and profligates, being chased and torn to pieces by dogs. In the inner ring are blasphemers and sodomites, residing in a desert of burning sand and burning rain falling from the sky. The seventh circle is serious stuff—between murderers and blasphemers. But then, so was Jesus on the cross.

The primary reason I do not subscribe to this belief, though, is not because of grace and forgiveness but because I do not believe in hell, at least not in the way most churches today describe it. Where did the hell of today's sermons come from? The church made it up.[17] Why? Power and control. It's the same kind of control that some attempt to assert today when they tell someone who's dealing with horrific physical or emotional pain, "If you end your own suffering, you will go to hell." Perhaps they will go to hell for lying.

Do We Die in God's Timing?

People who advocate this concept define God's timing as whenever you happen to die, unless you cause it, in which case it isn't God's timing; it's your timing, and you are not authorized to decide that for yourself. I often wonder what happened to their internal bullshit meters. I have more alarms ringing in my head when I hear this type of rhetoric than if I was in a military command center initiating DEFCON 5.

We only need to look to the life of Thomas Aquinas himself to dispel this idea. Pope Gregory X invoked a general council at Lyons on May 1, 1274. He invited Thomas and Bonaventure to take part in the deliberations, commanding the former to bring to the council his treatise *Contra errores Graecorum* (*Against the Errors of the Greeks*). Thomas, in ill health, set out on foot in January 1274. He fell to the ground near Terracina, from whence he was conducted to the Castle of Maienza, the home of his niece, the Countess Francesca Ceccano. When Father Reginald urged him to remain at the castle, Thomas replied, "If the Lord wishes to take me away, it is better that I be found in a religious house than in the dwelling of a lay person."[18] The Cistercian monks of Fossa Nuova pressed him to accept their hospitality, and he was conveyed to their monastery where he passed on March seventh of that year.

Thomas Aquinas hastened his own death. However, he did it in obedience to the church. Thus, it is argued that his death was still in God's timing and not of his own making. Of the seven suicides in the Bible, one of them shows Samson ending his life while taking out hundreds of Philistines. His suicide is treated differently from the other six under this concept because he also killed Israel's enemies at the same time. According to this logic, may Christians strap on an explosive vest and blow up a mosque? I find this thought both abhorrent and against my Christian beliefs.

Years ago, I read a story about a head-on collision between a particular half-ton import pickup and a big-block V-8 car. The driver and passenger of the pickup were dead by the time emergency vehicles reached the scene. What about those in the car? They sustained minor injuries. The names of the deceased were withheld in the story, pending notification of family members. Later in the day, I discovered that the driver of the pickup was a friend of mine on his way to an evangelistic crusade. I knew that he selected that pickup because of its economical gas mileage, and he believed his stewardship of God's money (donated to his ministry) required such a decision. I had disagreed with him, believing that other factors should also play a role. At the time, I drove a used Mercedes 300D, a fairly indestructible car. We paid about the same price for our vehicles. His truck got better mileage, yet it played a role in his death.

People speculated that God must have wanted him to die that way because he believed God wanted him to drive that truck. People said God spared the people in the other car because they were not yet saved. I denounced then (and still do today) both of those ideas. He died because he was behind the wheel of a tin can in a head-on collision with an anvil. God does not orchestrate death or so arrange events in this world that sinners die one way and saved people another.[19]

We are all going to die, and we all play a role in our own death through the choices we make, choices often starting before we even know enough information to make fully informed decisions. If the choices I make to honor God also bring about my death, I am called a saint. Yet if my final decision is purely to end my life on my terms, I am perceived as selfish, and my death is not in God's timing.

The truth is, there is no difference. We are the instruments of God in our own lives. If I intend to honor God by preaching at a revival but choices involved in that intention result in my death, proponents of this belief say it is an acceptable way to die. Why is it not acceptable for me to honor God in my dying intention?

There is no special place in hell reserved for people who commit suicide. Whether we participate in our own dying intentionally or unintentionally does not change what happens after we die. Setting aside these artificial reasons not to end your life, let us return to a true discussion of more realistic personal harm brought on by suicide.

Reasons against Suicide

Statistics vary, depending on the study quoted, yet the research agrees on one thing: if you attempt suicide, odds are you will not succeed.[20] Why does this matter? Fall off a bike, pick it up, and continue. Commit suicide and fail? Your world becomes a different place.

I studied suicide methods before my first attempt. I read stories about a man who used a gun and blew off the front of his face but did not die. Did his family members help him pick up his bike and give him a confidence boost? Just the opposite. He went through months of surgeries and physical therapy, all the time being monitored to ensure he would not be a danger to himself or anyone else. Other people use pills, don't die, and get rushed to a hospital. Now everyone is put on notice that the person made a suicide attempt, possibly including the person's employer.

My choice? Slit wrists in a bathtub of warm water, salts added to keep the wounds open. I watched as blood flowed out of each deeply cut wrist. I went to sleep, intending to never wake up. I do not know how much time passed, but I heard a voice: "Frank, wake up! Don't let her see you like this!" My eyes opened to dark red water, veins no longer bleeding, and my body ashen white. I bandaged my wrists, rinsed the tub, and went to bed. A few minutes later, my wife walked in. My world changed.

It never occurred to me I would not succeed. Yet while I lay too weak to even talk, she asked questions, and she felt scared. Her world changed as well; what she thought of as a secure relationship vaporized in minutes. Eventually my mental health issues drove us apart, and someone I thought I would be married to until the end of my life (how ironic is that?) needed to let me go.

People can lose jobs, relationships, health, honor, and self-esteem from a failed suicide attempt. No, this is not at all like falling off a bike when you are a kid. If you think you have problems now, your failed suicide only multiplies them. Unless you are terminally ill, American society (and most others) is not going to help you commit suicide. In fact, everyone will work harder to ensure you do not have another opportunity. I don't like that reality, but for now it is part of our experience.

If you are going to commit suicide, make sure you have a good plan and follow through successfully. If you don't like your life now, I am confident you will like it even less after an unsuccessful suicide attempt.[21] How certain are you that you are going to succeed? Does it bother you that most people who attempt suicide and fail—myself included—believed they would succeed?

Perhaps you are one of the successful ones. You're dead. Problems solved. Let me give you one more thing to think about. Did your suicide accomplish everything you wanted?

After my unsuccessful attempt, I came up with a plan I knew would succeed. I studied weapons, weapon placement, trajectory, ammo size, and trigger squeeze issues for a weapon pointed in the opposite direction of how it is designed to be used. I read dozens of failed suicide-by-weapon stories to learn what people did wrong.

I cared about my family, my unit, my mission, and my memory. Considering all the ramifications, I still wanted to end my life. I was tired of the pain, the pills, and the emotional roller coaster. Yes, I had made a lot of progress: physically, from not walking at all to using a cane, then walking unsupported, and then being able to run again (albeit not as well); emotionally, from living in an uncontrollable whirlwind to riding a roller coaster on which I could at least predict the tracks in a detached calm. Spiritually, I had regressed from a highpoint in my life, working on a chaplain team during my first deployment, to disappointment about my book's lack of action to feeling disconnection from any spiritual community that was once the most important part of my life. In fact, I felt detached from everything. After several months of planning my suicide, nothing surfaced to convince me to stop my preparations. I had no reason to live. Sometimes people die not because that is what they really want but because they can't figure out how to live. I felt at peace with my decision. A voice beckoned, saying, "This way and all will be well." Death is not the ultimate problem solver it pretends to be.

The following Friday, I sat in my trailer with hours at my disposal. According to a friend in the major's office, the range would go hot that day. "E-day," I told myself; at dinner time, when most of the troops would be at the dining facility, none of them waiting for me. The range would be finishing up with the sporadic shots of night fire qualifications. I went to the upper room but not for a last meal. I loaded a magazine into the well and chambered a round. The selector switch remained on *safe*. I sat down and then mentally walked through all the steps I had rehearsed dozens of times in my mind: weapon on the floor, angled back from under my chin to the back of my head, one hand holding the upper stocks, the other to rotate the selector switch and depress the trigger. End of story. Except it wasn't.

In late 2004, during my first Iraq deployment, my son sent an e-mail to me asking if I was okay and if I could find a way to call him. I did. He nearly cried for joy when he heard my voice. He told me that he had received a phone call from someone posing as a military member who told him that I had been killed in action. He told me how hard he cried, screamed into the air, and got angry at God. He couldn't deal with the news and was living an emotional nightmare until I called.

As I cradled the weapon in 2009, a vision of my son receiving the news flooded my mind. I could see him curled up in agony. I could hear his cries and feel his pain. The M16 shook in my hands, as if responding at the same time to a dual set of instructions. The control center in my brain continued issuing the order in the voice of a drill sergeant: "Move the selector switch from safe to semi, and squeeze the trigger." I did. With my thumb of my left hand steady on the trigger ready to push down, my right hand started shaking. If I fired, I might fail, cause irreparable damage, and still be alive. I tried to calm my right hand, but the vision of my son screaming at the news of my death wouldn't allow it. After several minutes of shaking, I laid the weapon down. Then my entire body began to shake.

I wanted to end my life for several reasons. One is that I felt like a failure as a father. I wanted something better for my kids. I hate myself for some of the decisions I made. I wanted to be a positive influence in their lives, but I didn't know how.

I also wanted an end to all my various physical, emotional, and spiritual pain. Suicide would have accomplished that. For several years afterward, I wished I had gone through with it. However, suicide was only an alternative because I didn't see another way to end any of it. Today I am a positive presence in my children's lives. I am happily married again, and my career is better than ever. I have more joy, peace, comfort, and love in my life than I ever thought possible. Today I am glad I did not succeed.

I challenge you to be honest with yourself. What do you really want? What do you think your suicide is going to accomplish? If you truly want an end to the madness, I get it. Suicide will get you there. However, if what you really want is connection or love or peace, suicide will not accomplish that. All suicide will do is ensure you never achieve what you really want.

This chapter is perhaps the most important. Feel free to stop reading here. You might have some thinking to do. Be honest with yourself. Perhaps reach out to a friend. Verify your assumptions. Read some stories and statistics. Pray. Mediate.

The remainder of this section discusses how suicide hurts our communities and nation. In the final section we will look at some reasons to live and how you can be in full control of your own future and create the life you want.

CHAPTER 2
COMMUNITY HARM

Our grief was more painful than anything we had known. My whole body literally ached for nearly two years after Daniel died. I felt as bruised as if I had been run over by a car. And along with the pain, there were the inevitable questions.

Would he still be alive if we had allowed him to go to the sleepover? Would he have survived if we had gotten him treatment for depression? Could we have stopped him from committing suicide if we had followed him into his room and talked to him after he had come home angry? What was he thinking in the moments before he died?

It is hard to avoid the conclusion that we failed our son. Even when we were assured by experts that suicide is the act of an irrational person, we kept thinking of things we could have done and words we could have uttered that might have prevented his death.[22]

I hesitate to write this section for several reasons. One is that writing it feels shameful and hypocritical, part of my soul believing that I am not worthy to do so. I knew my suicide plans would wound my social network and leave suicide survivors.

I also fear that some suicides will view this section as additional incentive to end their lives because their primary motivation for suicide is to inflict as much pain as possible on their survivors. I do not support this thought pattern and will deal with it momentarily.

Finally, I recognize that when I am most drawn to suicide, I do not want to consider the consequences of that action on others. For several years I did not want to discuss with anyone the anguish that taking my own life could inflict. My pain was already unbearable, and such parleys exacerbated my despair. If you are a suicidal and find yourself sinking into emotional turmoil from reading this part of the book, then please stop reading. Return to it when you are ready.

When was I ready? After three suicide episodes, I vowed to never attempt suicide again. However, PTSD-related anger issues increased until I became a real threat to my family— something I wanted to avoid by ending my life. After one nearly tragic incident, I wanted to end my life again despite all my promises. I knew that episode four would succeed. Instead of initiating my plan, I checked into a VA hospital and asked for help. I spent that night in a small, padded, fully observed room, shaking uncontrollably. I felt capable of facing the potential consequences of my suicide several months into the recovery process.[23]

An Alternative to Intentional Harm

Do you want to cause the most emotional harm you can to your family and friends? Suicide can accomplish that. The messier the better, with an incriminating note telling the world how it did not listen, didn't appreciate you, ostracized you, and abused you. I do not support suicide for the purpose of inflicting pain or violence on others. I do support the inherent right of individuals to determine their own lives and deaths. Ethical suicide[24] relieves suffering and does not multiply it.

You may believe your community deserves such heartache. Perhaps it does. You judge that they merit this turmoil because of the harm they did you. Can you see that you judge their actions as deserving of punishment, yet you are about to commit that very deed? You condemn harming others and judge that those who consciously inflict physical or emotional pain are deserving of such themselves. And yet you are about to inflict what you know will be an emotionally painful experience. This is hypocritical and will not accomplish its stated intentions. You are deceiving yourself, and your death will be in vain.

You may believe that in death you can accomplish something you never could in life: freeing yourself of people you do not like. You will accomplish that. However, if your social network is as dismissive of you as you believe, your death is not likely to harm them as much as you imagine. Your successful suicide will more likely be remembered by them as your ultimate failure than your crowning achievement.

If your community is so harmful to you, then leave. It's hard to do if one is a teenager or in the military, which may partially explain why suicide is more prevalent in those groups. Pursue your good, your health, and your passion. Reinvent yourself, even if it takes years. You may find your ultimate success more of a continuous thorn in their souls than your death could ever be.[25]

Suicide Inevitably Harms

Perhaps you realize your suicide will harm those you care about, yet you are just done with life. I get that. Before you pull the trigger on your plan, though, I want you to consider the consequences your death might have on those who care about you the most.

My wife (at the time) viewed me and our relationship differently after my first attempt. She had not foreseen that "till death do us part" could include such an early, premeditated departure. Yes, my life insurance would pay off the house and provide for several years. But I had concealed the extent of my emotional despair from her, the one I said I fully trusted. My suicide clearly demonstrated my values of solving my issues my way rather than working together. Our relationship never recovered.

If my suicide plan had succeeded, our relationship would have ended, so why did our breakup affect me so deeply? I loved her and thought that my death would help her. She didn't see the benefit to her, only the pain. And I could see it in her face.

Grieving the death of a loved one is one of the hardest emotional human experiences. When that death is a suicide, betrayal and other issues are added to grieving, making suicide survival (in my mind) perhaps the toughest human experience to endure. Based on my experiential evidence, I see surviving a suicide as more dangerous than surviving any other death of a loved one. This is not an accident with no one to blame; this is not a murder perpetrated by someone outside the community circle. A suicide is a combination of the individual's issues and the network's responses—joint perpetrators within the community circle.

Suicide survivors often feel shame, guilt, and a lack of closure. The death is rarely talked about, if at all, with pride in the way someone might discuss the death of a military member in the line of duty. To some survivors (who never previously entertained such an idea) suicide can become appealing as a way to resolve their heartaches. I am not interested in parading survivor stories to prove that suicide uniquely harms a suicidal's social network. The Internet is full of such stories,[26] and several books provide numerous survivor stories.[27]

Instead of survivor stories, I want to include here a brief summary of a research survey. Referring to research does not suggest that scientific research provides a better understanding of suicide than personal observations. Clinical research and practical observations are both important to help us understand the reasons and results of people choosing to end their lives.

What We Know about Social Impact

Blame. Suicide survivors judge themselves more negatively than survivors of other types of loss. They may be more disturbed and see themselves as more deserving of blame for the suicide. Blame can be overtly and covertly communicated. Blame dissolves family cohesiveness. Even if survivors conclude that they are not responsible for the suicide, many struggle with their perceived failure to intervene.

Secrecy. Survivors tend to conceal the cause of death. Although survivors are reported as being asked to provide details about the suicide more often than other types of death, I wonder if this is because they tune into such questions more (such as buying a new car and then seeing them everywhere) or because society in general knows better how to process, say, heart attacks. Secrecy subtly plays with family dynamics as well. Some want to keep the self-inflicted part out of the story if possible to preserve family honor, while others feel a need to talk about it so they can heal.

Ostracizing. Sometimes people who get divorced find that their married friends don't want to socialize with them, as if they have a contagious disease. Having a member of a family commit suicide is more ostracizing than divorce. Although the stigma of suicide is decreasing, survivors still report feeling ostracized by their social networks. They also tend to exclude themselves from social situations if they are uncomfortable with or do not know how to address the suicide as a potential topic of conversation.

Ripples. Survivors report marijuana use, alcohol misuse, suicidal ideation and attempts, inflicting severe injuries, and emotional distress. Daniel's mother reported thinking of suicide several times. Realizing that I would leave a suicide legacy for my kids played a huge role in my decision to move off my suicide path.

Let's Get Personal

I want to connect with suicidals directly for a moment. I designed the following exercise to help you realize the impact your suicide might have on people who care about you. Please proceed when you are by yourself in a safe environment.

Picture someone you care about—someone living, someone who also cares about you. It could be a spouse, a child, a family member, a dear friend, your BFF (best friend forever), or your MSP (most special person). Think about him or her for a moment. Think of memories that make the person special to you. Hold those thoughts for a moment.

Now imagine a car pulling up in front of your home. Two people in professional attire walk to the door. They introduce themselves as police department casualty assistance officers. They ask if they may come in. They ask you to sit down. You demand to know what they want, afraid of bad news. They ask you again to sit down. You do. They tell you that your MSP was brutally murdered.

Feel your response to this news. You feel angry, sad, and hopeless. There is searing emotional pain and heartache so strong that physical symptoms quickly follow. An emotional earthquake has happened at the epicenter of your life, and the columns supporting your social framework crumble around you. Soon you experience shortness of breath, dizziness, and weakness in your legs. You want to scream or cry. You demand justice. A guilty verdict can bring a sense of closure, and you desperately need that right now, although it won't come fast enough. You want to know how and why it happened and what they are doing to find the murderer.

Stay with those emotions for a minute. Now pause, and take a deep breath. It did not happen; your friend hasn't been murdered. Picture your MSP again and some different memories you hold dear. Stay with these memories until you return to serene feelings.

Now imagine your MSP at home. Maybe it is also your home, but you are not there. A vehicle pulls up. Two people in professional attire approach the door. They introduce themselves and ask to come in.

This time the news is not about murder but your suicide. How might your MSP feel? Is there the same searing emotional pain and physiological symptoms? Definitely. But there's no demand for justice.

Instead of justice, there is perhaps betrayal, guilt, or shame. There is no definitive closure for these types of feelings.

Can you see the pain in the person's eyes, facial expressions, and body language? That is the beginning of the impact your suicide will have on him or her.

There is more in store for the MSP, as the study referenced above indicates, but this is enough to consider for now. Come back to being present in your surroundings. Breathe.

What do you want regarding your MSP or your social network? If your relationships are so broken that you contemplate ending the pain by taking your own life and yet what you really want is connection, I can show you a way to restore yourself within your social fabric. Will you try my recommendations first? For their sakes and yours.

CHAPTER 3

NATIONAL HARM

Americans are far more likely to kill themselves than each other. Homicides have fallen by half since 1991, but the U.S. suicide rate keeps climbing. The nearly 40,000 American lives lost each year make suicide the nation's 10th-leading cause of death, and the second-leading killer for those ages 15–34. Each suicide costs society about $1 million in medical and lost-work expenses and emotionally victimizes an average of 10 other people. Yet a national effort to stem this raging river of self-destruction — 90 percent of which occurs among Americans suffering mental illness — is in disarray.[28]

Approximately one million individuals worldwide died by suicide in 2000, and estimates suggest that 10 to 20 times more individuals attempted suicide. Only two interventions have been shown to prevent deaths by suicide and only one form of psychotherapy has been shown to prevent suicide attempts in more than one clinical trial. Why is the state of knowledge for such a devastating psychological phenomenon relatively lacking?[29]

Gregg Zoroya's article on suicide (first quote above) is a good introduction to a plethora of issues raised by suicide. While Zoroya accurately reports common statistics about suicide, I doubt that each suicide costs the nation over $1 million (what exactly is lost-work expenses?[30]). I also disagree with the characterization that suicide is a raging river of self-destruction. Sometimes suicide is the most compassionate outcome for all concerned. I fully agree with Zoroya, however, that suicide is a financial and emotional drain on our country.

If one could weave a tapestry that represents the soul of a state or nation, would suicide be noticeable? My design for a tapestry about the people of the United States includes depicting our nearly two hundred nationalities,[31] with all their passions, entertainment, livelihood,[32] creeds, and how they die.[33] If the size of each picture in the tapestry is proportional to its numbers, suicide is barely visible—a few threads at most in the largest tapestry I can imagine. Sometimes I envision suicide not as a picture at all but as an unraveling, loose thread that threatens the fabric or soul of our nation. Suicide is a wound, crimson drops of blood staining the vibrant colors of our collective life.

The government does not look at suicide this way.[34] To the powers that govern, suicide is primarily a financial and political issue rather than an emotional or moral issue. A brief historical review of the political state's view of suicide can help us understand both how we arrived at our current combination of rules and ethics and some approaches to suicide we might want to consider.

The Greek city-states did not have a national suicide policy. While Plato opposed suicide, he made three important exceptions: when ordered by the state (as in the case of Socrates), for painful or incurable illness, and when one is compelled by intolerable misfortune. The later relates to the Stoic philosophy of self-preservation of the rational being. To the Stoics, a life lived according to principle was more to be desired than mere life in any form. The Stoics preferred ending life as a rational being. It was considered to be the most or only rational act available.[35]

During the Roman Empire, citizens wanting to end their lives could apply to the Roman Senate for hemlock. Suicide was specifically forbidden to soldiers, slaves, and those accused of capital crimes. These were all purely economic categories. Rome confiscated the property of those convicted of capital crimes, so if the accused killed himself or herself prior to conviction, the state lost the right to seize the dead person's property. Emperor Domitian (81–96 CE) decreed that those who died prior to trial were without legal heirs, a handy legal device for an empire in need of funds for its endless military campaigns. I imagine that Rome did not accuse people of capital crimes, leave them to die or commit suicide in horrendous jails while awaiting trial, and then confiscate their property just because they needed funds. In the US, with our pleasant jails and long life spans, we don't need to wait for people to die or get convicted to confiscate their property. We just accuse them of drug crimes.[36]

The early Christian church provided food and alms to the families of martyrs; it was sometimes an economic incentive to poor Christians. Early Christian stories pointed to martyrs as precious in God's sight. Stephen was granted a glorious vision of heaven before he died. In the vision he saw Jesus standing at the right hand of the God the Father, waiting for Stephen in honor for his faithful service.[37] The writer of Revelation portrays those martyred for their faith reigning with Christ for a thousand years.[38] The apostle Peter, who wrote the most about martyrdom and suffering for one's faith, said, "If you are reviled for the name of Christ, you are blessed, because the Spirit of glory and of God rests on you ... but if anyone suffers as a Christian, he is not to be ashamed, but is to glorify God in this name."[39] Jesus blessed those persecuted for his name: "Blessed are you when people insult you and persecute you, and falsely say all kinds of evil against you because of Me."[40] Martyrdom appealed enough to early Christians that many sought it as a means to leave their earthly existences.

Tens of thousands of Christians voluntarily sought martyrdom in the first three centuries; others practiced strict asceticism that led to an early death. Everyone received honor from the Christian community and hope of additional favors in the afterlife. Following George Colt's chronicles of early Christian suicides, he concludes, "Clearly, things were getting out of hand."[41] Not surprisingly, teachings changed.

Timothy of Alexandria (ca. 372 CE) asked and answered the question, "If anyone having no control of himself lays violent hands on himself or hurls himself to destruction, whether an offering ought to be made for him or not?" Answer:

> The Clergyman ought to discern in his behalf whether he was actually and truly out of his mind when he did it. For oftentimes those who are interested in the victim and want to have him accorded an offering and a prayer in his behalf will deliberately lie and assert that he had no control of himself. Sometimes, however, he did it as a result of influence exercised by other men, or somehow otherwise as a result of paying too little attention to circumstances, and no offering ought to be made in his behalf. It is incumbent, therefore, upon the Clergyman in any case to investigate the matter accurately, in order to avoid incurring judgment. [42]

The offering in this case meant supplication by the clergy to God to receive that person's soul into heaven. Although addressed to the clergy, we see in this answer willingness by church leadership to extend its favor to suicides without mental capacity but not to those who purposefully choose suicide. Timothy of Alexandria's canons received ecumenical status by ratification in the Quinisext Synod in 692 CE.

Augustine published his *City of God* in 426 CE. Book I criticizes the pagans who attribute the sack of Rome to Christianity, explains why good and bad things happen to righteous and wicked people alike, and consoles Christian women violated in war. Several chapters in Book I deal with suicide. While sympathizing with virgins who killed themselves rather than be raped by the invading army, Augustine states that all suicide is murder. He does not discuss mental capacity, nor does he hold that rigorous piety leading more gradually to death is suicide. Social and religious conditions framing Augustine's writings are beyond the scope of this book and are covered elsewhere.[43]

Augustine also argues that lack of burial (i.e., bodies of Christians left on the battle field) did not defeat the opportunity for resurrection. A few centuries later, the church started denying burial rites to suicides (not always with regard to mental capacity) in terms of both religious ceremony and consecrated ground. In civil governments the bodies of suicides came to be treated the same as murderers, often hung or burned, even though they were already dead.

We also see through the centuries a battle between the church and civil authorities over the property of suicides. In some eras the church allowed suicides to leave property to the church as alms for good works done in their names to earn God's favor for them in purgatory. At other times, usually when the church denied burial rites, the civil authority confiscated a suicide's property to pay for burial expenses and debts. Burials were likely as inexpensive as possible, and excess funds kept rather than distributed to heirs.

Martin Luther (1483–1546) is one of my favorite characters of the Reformation era. His views on suicide also parted ways with Catholic theology that maintained all suicides are damned. He wrote, "It is very certain that, as to all persons who have hanged themselves, or killed themselves in any other way, 'tis the devil who has put the cords around their necks, or the knife to their throats."[44]

Suicides were not murderers, he argued; they have been murdered. Their eternal fate rested not in the type of death they suffered but whether or not, in life, they lived by faith.

Dr. Luther parts ways with Augustine on the suicide of young women facing potential harm. Someone asked him whether a young woman who killed herself by jumping out of a window rather than face violence about to be done by a nobleman was responsible for her own death. He replied, "No; she felt that this step formed her only chance of safety, it being not her life she sought to save, but her chastity."[45] I see in this inquiry the real question: will God damn her as a murderer?

Dr. Luther was also a product of his times. He saw demons in trees, water, and dark clouds; they tormented Christians at every opportunity. He viewed his own maladies as inflicted by demons rather than natural causes. People could spit on demons, chase them, rebuke them, or tear off a horn. Devils were male or female and could produce children through interactions with humans. Devils could act on people externally in myriad ways or internally through possession.

If people have suicidal thoughts, does this demonstrate a demon acting externally, like the little demons on their shoulders, whispering thoughts into their ears, or internally, possessing their minds and causing their bodies to obey commands the rational mind does not want to obey?

Today we view such discussions at best as playful exercises, no longer considering them to be plausible explanations. One day I hope people will look back on our current discussions of suicide as caused by mental illness as equally excusable ignorance.

The church faded as a ruling political power and with that decline came a decrease in treatment in clergy-run facilities. Care in the church-sponsored model had been generally humane. A daily routine for those in care included prayers, supplications, good works, and plenty of personal contact. These institutions could not treat the entire mentally ill population.

State asylums were established in the sixteenth century to accommodate the burgeoning numbers of mentally ill individuals. Asylums were not facilities aimed at helping the mentally ill overcome their illnesses. Instead, asylums were merely reformed penal facilities where the mentally ill were abandoned by relatives or sentenced to by the law. They faced lives of deplorable living conditions and cruel abuse. People with suicidal thoughts could be sent away by social networks that either could not or would not deal with their issues.

Many asylums were staffed by untrained, unqualified individuals. La Bicetre, a hospital in Paris, shackled patients to the wall in dark, cramped cells. Iron cuffs and collars permitted enough movement to allow patients to feed themselves but not enough to lie down at night. Straw covered the cold floors, and inmates were forced to sit in their own waste. The quality of the food or whether or not patients were adequately fed did not concern asylum staff. Visitors could only deliver food; no personal interactions were allowed. These conditions were not unique to La Bicetre. My favorite textbook from my psychology undergraduate years, *Abnormal Psychology*, paints a fairly accurate picture of a typical scene in asylums around the world from approximately the 1500s to the early 1900s.[46]

Some asylums did attempt to cure patients. Typical practices included purging, bloodletting, dousing the patient in either hot or ice-cold water, blistering, physical restraints, threats, or straitjackets.

In 1792, Philippe Pinel took charge of La Bicetre to test his hypothesis that mentally ill patients would improve if they were treated with kindness and consideration. Filth, noise, and abuse were eliminated, and patients were unchained. Rooms provided sunlight, and patients were allowed to exercise freely on the asylum grounds.

The York Retreat, founded in 1796 by Quakers in York, England, stressed the importance of treating the mentally ill with respect and compassion. The Retreat, a pleasant country house, allowed patients to live, work, and rest in a warm, religious environment that emphasized mildness, reason, and humanity.

An asylum in Devon, England, treated patients with exercise, recreation, diversified amusements, books for reflection (to be read out loud), and occupations of service, music, and properly trained attendants. Devon annual reports showed a shift from the end goal of "cure" to "recover." [47] It was a shift I view as a realization that we do not cure mental issues, as we might a medical malady, but we teach people skills to manage their lives.

Reform movements in the US at that time focused on abolition and temperance. Mental health reform received the attention it needed because of a school headmistress and children's book author suffering from tuberculosis. In 1836 Dorothea Dix closed her school for girls to travel to England in search of treatment. The Quaker family she stayed with introduced her to other Quakers who were active in mental health reform efforts. After returning to her home in Massachusetts in 1840, she conducted a statewide investigation of mental health institutions. Dix published her findings to the legislature in a scathing forty-four-page document titled *Memorial*.[48] Massachusetts expanded its state-run facility as a result.

Dix traveled to other states in an investigative capacity and submitted similar reports. Based on her recommendations, some responded by opening their first state-sponsored institutions. In 1854, Dix proposed an idea to the US Congress to initiate federally funded facilities. Her bill passed both the House and the Senate but was vetoed by President Franklin Pierce, a Democrat, who believed that social welfare was a state—not a federal—concern.

In 1887, then penniless Elizabeth Cochran accepted an assignment at Pulitzer's *World* newspaper in New York to gain admittance into the Women's Lunatic Asylum on Blackwell's Island, the first municipal institution in the country. Her goal was to investigate allegations of neglect and brutality. Cochran practiced gestures, such as pulling her own hair, and then checked into a boarding house under the name *Nellie Bly*. Refusing to go to bed and telling others they looked insane earned her a visit from the local police. A judge sent her to Bellevue Hospital for evaluation. Several doctors unanimously pronounced her insane and committed her to the asylum where Cochran met several women she deemed as sane as herself.

I find that if one really wants to discern the sane from the insane, it is often better to ask the patients than the doctors. Collectively, they know who they are. There is some truth, if not sanity, in Edgar Allen Poe's 1856 story, *The System of Doctor Tarr and Professor Fether*,[49] where a stranded traveler learns hidden secrets of a local asylum.

Cochran wrote several articles about her experiences in the asylum. The food consisted of gruel, broth, spoiled beef, and bread that was little more than dried dough. The drinking water was dirty, not fit for human consumption. The patients were made to sit for much of each day on hard benches with scant protection from the cold. Patients deemed violent were tied together with ropes. With waste littering the eating places, rats scurried freely around the hospital. The bathwater was frigid, and buckets of it were poured over inmates' heads for showers. The nurses were obnoxious and abusive, yelling at the patients to shut up, beating them if they did not. As for her own experience, I paused when I read her comment that "It is only after one is in trouble that one realizes how little sympathy and kindness there are in the world." [50]

A grand jury investigated her reports. The city of New York increased its budget for the asylum by $850,000 and instituted numerous system reforms. Today Blackwell Island is Roosevelt Island, a prominent residential strip under the Queensboro Bridge. All that remains of the former asylum is the octagonal tower that made up the center of the original building; it entered the national register of historic places in 1972 and was restored as part of a modern apartment complex. I wonder whether the complex houses more truly insane people than the original asylum (although we would not call them that as long as they pay their rent and don't disturb their neighbors).

One of my favorite mental health historical figures is John Harvey Kellogg (1852–1943). While some today correctly connect his name with Kellogg's Corn Flakes, many do not know that he developed the cereal while he was the chief medical officer for the Battle Creek Sanitarium. He did so in part to solve the typical lack of nutrition issues extant in preparing food for large populations. Patients at Battle Creek received a low-fat, low-protein diet with an emphasis on whole grains, fiber-rich foods, and nuts. The sanitarium also emphasized a daily intake of fresh air, exercise, and good hygiene. Services provided for its private-pay clients included hydrotherapy, phototherapy, thermotherapy, electrotherapy, mechanotherapy, dietetics, physical culture, cold-air cure, and health training. The sanitarium is now the Hart-Dole-Inouye Federal Center. Why we name buildings for Senators just because they are good at spending other people's money to acquire buildings is beyond my mental grasp.

Kellogg believed that mental health issues are a result of refusing to deal with sin in one's life. Kellogg believed that "self-abuse" (masturbation) caused most of the mental illness he witnessed. The one suicide mentioned in his book, *Plain Facts*, happened shortly after the person was released from the sanitarium. Admitted for behaviors that left the patient greatly emaciated, Dr. Kellogg diagnosed the cause of his ailment as the guilt consequence of self-abuse and recommended stopping that activity, noting, "He promised to reform; but if he did, it was too late, for the wasting disease which was fastened upon him continued." A few weeks after returning home, the young man ended his life with a pistol.[51]

We still believe that guilt can play a part in the development of mental health issues, although we might disagree with the extent self-abuse is actually as significant a factor as Kellogg claimed. Perhaps the stigma placed on certain behaviors is more salient than the behavior itself.

In 1900 Clifford Beers was first confined to a private mental institution for depression and paranoia. He would later be confined to another private hospital and a state institution. During these periods he experienced and witnessed serious maltreatment at the hands of the staff. His book, *A Mind That Found Itself*, chronicled his hospitalization and the abuses he suffered.[52] Rather than just criticizing the mental health profession, he worked with it to reform the treatment of the mentally ill. In 1909, Beers founded the National Committee for Mental Hygiene to continue reforming for treatment of the mentally ill.

Even with the best intentions of the mental health reform movement, schizophrenia and other persistent mental illnesses were treated with drugs, electroconvulsive therapy, and surgery. Some were infected with malaria; others were treated with repeated insulin-induced comas. Lobotomies, surgically removing parts of the brain, became a common treatment for schizophrenia, depression, severe anxiety, and obsessions. In the 1930s and 1940s doctors experimented with convulsions induced by the injection of camphor or electroshock therapy.

On July 3, 1946, President Harry Truman, also a Democrat, reversed President Pierce's decision and made mental health the business of the federal government by signing into law the National Mental Health Act, calling for a National Institute of Mental Health (NIMH) to conduct research into the brain and reduce mental illness.[53]

The number of people hospitalized for mental health issues continued to climb through the mid-1950s. Hospitalization as a treatment protocol started to decline as behavior-based therapies and self-administered drug treatments arose. Behavior therapy combined the principles of classical conditioning developed by Ivan Pavlov and operant conditioning developed by B.F. Skinner.

In 1960 psychiatrist Thomas Szasz wrote an essay titled *The Myth of Mental Illness*. Expanded into a book published the following year, the essay argued that "Our adversaries are not demons, witches, fate, or mental illness. We have no enemy whom we can fight, exorcise, or dispel by 'cure.' What we do have are problems in living."[54]

While Szasz's books continue to positively impact people who were designated as having mental illness, the reaction from the mental health community, in my judgment, did not acknowledge his proposals but instead entrenched itself in order to justify access to millions of federal dollars.[55]

During the late 1950s sociologist Erving Goffman studied the behavior of institutionalized patients. He wrote four essays, collectively published in the 1961 book *Asylums*.[56] Lacking a generally accepted scientific method and containing many overly-broad generalizations,[57] his work significantly influenced the deinstitutionalization movement. The early 1960s marked a significant shift of patients from institutions to community-based solutions.

On October 31, 1963, President John F. Kennedy signed into law the Community Mental Health Act (also known as the Mental Retardation and Community Mental Health Centers Construction Act of 1963), which provided the first federal money for developing a network of community-based mental health services. Deinstitutionalization's success needed people with mental illness to voluntarily seek out treatment at these facilities. Although successful for a period of time in which the negative images of institutionalization remained, community solutions eventually proved to be no viable solution either.

When I discuss current issues in mental illness, many in the profession state that today's problems started with Ronald Reagan closing all the institutions in 1980 and tossing mentally ill people into the streets. I have heard that phrase repeated so many times I wonder to what extent it is a mere mantra within parts of the profession. It should come as no surprise to readers that I do not accept this assertion as the whole story of how we arrived at our current dilemma.

During my final year of law school in early 2003, many classmates praised Governor George Ryan (R) when he eliminated the death penalty in Illinois and commuted the existing death penalty sentences of 167 inmates to life without parole. Having investigated the death penalty process in his state for three years, he concluded that the numerous injustices in the system required this blanket action. Is that what Ronald Reagan did in 1981—commute the sentences of all institutionalized mentally ill patients to life on the streets? No.

In the news at the time of this writing is a House budget proposal designed to stop President Obama's executive orders on certain immigration issues. Tied to the budget for Homeland Security, a proposed amendment would end a 2012 program that offers safe harbor to young people brought to the US illegally as children and subject six hundred thousand people in the program to deportation. Is that what Ronald Reagan did by directly stopping the funding of mental health institutions so that they would be forced to release their patients? Again, no.

Reagan's Omnibus Budget Reconciliation Act of 1981 repealed Carter's Mental Health Systems Act of 1980 and consolidated treatment and rehabilitation service programs into a single block grant administered by the states. The federal role in services to the mentally ill became one of providing technical assistance, allowing states to increase the capacity of local providers. True, the funds in the consolidated program was less than the amount allocated to mental health services in Carter's bill, but the prevalent theory at the time predicted that state-run programs would be more effective and cost less overall than the federal service model. The results didn't work out as anticipated, but I do not blame President Reagan for the results.[58]

In 1999 David Satcher, then US Surgeon General, published a call to action to address the public health issue of suicide.[59] The proposal included fifteen key recommendations that support a new, comprehensive national strategy for suicide prevention. I find that his proposals, based on input from numerous organizations and conferences, paints a

realistic picture of the influences on suicide and how to address those issues at local, state, and national levels. As a sergeant in the Washington
Army National Guard at the time, I experienced the call to action by
attending a mandatory suicide prevention class. At the time I did not
sense the importance of the class or why I needed to spend drill weekend hours in such discussions.

Just before my first deployment to Iraq in 2008, the US Army announced a $50 million study on suicide and suicide behavior in the
military under the direction of the National Institute of Mental Health.
On hearing the news, one of my friends said, "I can save the Army $50
million. Stop deploying people to stupid wars!" I nodded, although
I doubted that her recommendation would be considered. The real
purpose of the study, in my opinion, was to find a way to continue
deploying people at the whim of the US government without further
provoking family members who were writing nasty letters to their
Congressmen demanding that they do something about the high number of military suicides.

The history of mental illness and suicide is broader than this short
survey can cover.[60] My intention with this section is to provide background for my observation about seeing mental health issues through
the eyes of the government. When I look through those eyes, I see a
system more concerned about its own image, its budget, its bureaucratic
territories, its reelection, its public employee union contracts, and man-
agement of its citizens than about actually creating a framework for
true mental health. Mental health practitioners also play a role in this
concern when they defend their administrative territory or historical
claims even though evidence continues to mount that psychotherapy
and other forms of intervention are not a solution.

Often overlooked in the mental health discussion are the rights of
individuals themselves. To what extent do we, as citizens of our states
and voters of our own government, want government to be able to
incarcerate us simply by declaring that we have a mental disease that
a growing body of science believes does not exist? We, as communities
and individuals, gave this power to our governing bodies as we threw

our hands in the air and claimed we did not know what to do. Our lives are better off when that crazy family member isn't around; let the state take care of him or her. This too is part of the reason suicide continues to be a national issue.

I am not, though, one to simply point fingers and walk away from the discussion; merely passing judgment accomplishes nothing.

PART 3

SUICIDE'S
SOLUTIONS

CHAPTER 1
PERSONAL SOLUTIONS

Men do not attract that which they want, but that which they are. Their whims, fancies, and ambitions are thwarted at every step, but their inmost thoughts and desires are fed with their own food, be it foul or clean. The "divinity that shapes our ends" is in ourselves; it is our very self. Only himself manacles man: thought and action are the gaolers of Fate—they imprison, being base; they are also the angels of Freedom—they liberate, being noble. Not what he wishes and prays for does a man get, but what he justly earns. His wishes and prayers are only gratified and answered when they harmonize with his thoughts and actions.[61]

I looked at what I was attracting into my life and I asked myself the question "Who am I, that I am attracting this into my life: the aloneness, the isolation, the poverty, the different ways that I showed up in the world?" I learned to change that.[62]

Let's have a chat, you and I. I realize that you do not know me. This is because you are reading my words, so the passion in my eyes and facial expressions remain unseen. It is also because, for most of my life, I did not allow people to get to know me. You already know the problems created by suicide, yet you hold fast to the potential benefits of your death. Your issues more real than others admit; they are problems so seemingly insurmountable that death is a release, a gift, a way out.

What if there is another way? Not drugs, numbing your mind until there is nothing left of your personality. Not confinement, increasing your anger as your body is restrained from acting on the commands given it by your mind. Instead, a transformation into the life you really want to live. I lived it and saw it happen dozens of times as I share these ideas with others. You are the miracle you have been waiting for. The life experience you've seen, wanted, and had ripped from you are still waiting for you to claim.

This chapter is the most important one in the book for me. Strengthening networks and discussing public policy is important but not as important to me as you restoring your life to everything you want it to be. When I meet persons dealing with suicidal thoughts, I want them to hear several things from me: I care about them, I support them in whatever they are going through, and I want them to consider the benefits and damage of their decision. Mostly I just listen.

I am not a therapist and do not take on that role. However, I occasionally help suicidals restore their lives, as I did my own. Some suicidals do not feel safe seeing a mental health professional or do not have the means to pay for such services. Others want to break free from, rather than cope with, the patterns of depression, anger, shame, hopelessness that lead them to suicide. They deserve to live lives that are fulfilling, loving, compassionate, peaceful, joyful, grateful, abundant, hopeful, and rewarding.

I wish I could see your eyes right now. Some people look away when I tell them about the lives they deserve. They don't believe it. They believe that if I knew what they did, or went through, I wouldn't believe it either. I have not yet heard a story from a suicidal that stops me from believing the truth about him or her.

Maybe you don't see it yet, so borrow some faith from me. You deserve the life you want to live, and it is possible to create it. Period. That applies no matter who you are or what you did or went through. Your life can be restored to you, just as mine was. You just need to take the first step, then the next, and then the next. It's one step at a time.

Others want you to step into your own life. You bring unique skills this world desperately needs right now. How do I know this? For starters, you hold a high regard for life. Non-suicidals often don't un-derstand this. They believe choosing to end existence indicates a strong disregard for life. They fail to grasp that part of our motivation stems from recognizing a life we want to live, a life that seems to permanent evade us. I discovered that our projections are self-fulfilling prophecies. They are only as correct as we want them to be. What if you could live the life you want? It's a triple win because you, your community, and your country will benefit.

The following steps or skills can be tapped into whenever needed. Pick up the tools as and when you need them. Add others. Build your own survivor kit. While many of the actions below are now a habit for me, I still consciously choose to focus on these attributes and continue honing their effectiveness. Do not worry if your current skill level with any of them is zero. It's where many of us start. With a few of these I felt as if I was looking up at zero from inside a dark well. The good news is that, with even a small success or step forward, you are no longer at zero.

View Suicide as a Spectrum

If you have been to any counseling or therapy for suicide, you may have seen one of several variations of this abbreviated suicide spectrum chart:

Risk Level	Ideology	Action
Low	Is not preoccupied with death, has normal thoughts of one's own mortality	None
Mild	Morbid preoccupation with death, does not have a plan	Requires referral
Medium	Considered a method, no current plan	Requires immediate referral
High	Has a current plan	Contact MH immediately; do not leave suicidal alone.

I want to change the way we think about suicide as a spectrum. The chart above is useful for mental health and social workers but not so helpful for suicidals or communities because it leaves us totally out of the picture in the action plan.

Here is how I see suicide as a spectrum:

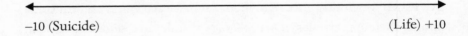

–10 (Suicide)   (Life) +10

Suicide is not all or nothing. You may hear people say that part of them died when something happened. Others may say they allowed a part of them to die, such as an old habit, and a new self emerged. Not all death is negative. As an overgrown forest may need a fire to survive and as seeds die to create plants, so too we may need to put part of our selves to death to fully live. Let's say you have no plan to end your life and are not preoccupied with morbid thoughts of death. Where are you on the chart? "None." The system has no action plan for you; the system has other suicidals to attend to. You need to create your own plan to move toward your definition of a +10 life.

Each spectrum is unique. The spectrum is not filled in with details about–4 or +5 because you are unique. Life at –8 for you is different than –8 for me. Moving from –8 to –7 will require different steps for each of us. Your MH professional or support community may leave you at –8, thinking that, as long as you are not at –10, they've done their job. Life can be scary at –8. Some employers don't want to hire you. Friends may avoid you, as if you have a contagious disease. This is not a spot on the spectrum where you want to stay.

Emotions are not on the spectrum. For most of my life I blocked feeling what I considered negative emotions. We may hear messages such as *Don't cry,* while we rarely hear *Don't laugh.* We might even hear *I'll give you something to cry about.* Fortunately, our social construct around emotions is changing in healthy ways, and we now know that an emotional reaction to an experience is what it is—neither positive nor negative. How we respond, including the stories we tell ourselves, moves us along the spectrum toward life or toward death. Allow yourself to feel your emotions, including your pain. Then consciously move in the direction that adds life.

Say yes to + (positive) activities. When I chose life and made a commitment to no longer consider plans to end my life, I viewed my life at a –8 on the spectrum. I did not immediately find myself returning to the full life of +10. If I describe my day as a –6 or +7, that does not mean every experience in that day was that number. The number is an average. People are amazingly complex, capable of having a +10 moment in the midst of a day filled with –6 emotions. Be grateful for the +10 moment; cherish it. Find ways to add such moments to your life. What do you like to do? What makes you happy? What gives you energy? What is your passion? If someone you like to spend time with offers to share a + experience with you, say yes. If someone asks you how your day was and your answer is –6, don't launch into a story about the strong negatives. What positive experiences brought your day up to a −6? As we focus on the positive experiences in our lives we attract more of them.

Say no to – (negative) activities. In grade school grammar we learned that a double negative is a positive. The sentence *He never does nothing* is understood to mean *He is always doing something.* Saying no to a negative activity in your life is a positive choice. Is this activity or this substance you are putting into your body or this story you are telling yourself, or the influence of this person in your life moving you in the direction of death? Have the courage to say no, and stick to your decision. Create support around that decision with your community. Your life is now headed in a different direction. Replace that activity, that substance, that story, and that person with one that will move you in the other direction.

Avoid Avoidance

Avoidance can be a healthy behavior. I prefer to avoid snakes and bears when I am hiking, people with guns and knives in dark alleys, and drunk drivers on highways. Avoidance can also be unhealthy, leading to mistrust, taking offense easily, having difficulty with forgiveness, assuming a defensive attitude in response to imagined criticism, being preoccupied with hidden motives, feeling fear of being deceived or taken advantage of, or experiencing an inability to relax.

When I felt anxiety mounting in the past, I avoided whatever created the tension. I left the first post-deployment July Fourth celebration after only a few minutes of fireworks. It was disturbing to hear the sounds of launching fireworks through mortar tubes and a loud bang followed by flashes of light. I began to avoid crowded areas such as malls, movie theaters on busy weekends, and traffic where I had no maneuver room. Eventually I avoided nearly everything, walking downtown streets late at night but mostly staying in my sparsely furnished apartment. I rarely invited people over. The few granted access would comment, "It looks like no one even lives here."

Some people don't like galleries of modern art, so they don't visit them. That is not unhealthy avoidance, although they miss out on a fabulous cultural opportunity. Since no one knows what modern art is supposed to represent, or whether it represents anything at all, one can, with the right mix of confidence, tone, facial expression, and sophisticated phrases stolen from others, come across as a connoisseur and knowledgeable critic of nothing at all. One does not need a mental illness to avoid reality; sophistication (even if assumed) accomplishes the same thing without the stigma of paranoia.

I did not avoid conflict in Iraq. One day, at a meeting at the chapel on our base, mortars landed just outside the building. Most of the soldiers dropped, as they are trained to do. I went down to one knee, watched, listened, and counted. We developed a theory in the intel office that if we counted six seconds after a mortar, that was the last one. Whoever launched mortars at that time did so quickly and left. Several mortars fell, with only a few seconds between them. When I reached six, I darted out the door to the impact area to look for anyone needing aid. I do not have a history of shirking from danger.

Yet for two years of my life I avoided everything. My legal practice dwindled, and my health declined. Friendships disintegrated not because people didn't care but because they did not know what to do. I promised my doctor and a few close friends that I would call if I became suicidal again. I never called. Every night I prayed the prayer in the beginning of this book, mad at God that if he wasn't going to end my life (having survived two previous attempts that seemed to indicate divine intervention), then at least he could take my life so I wouldn't have to. Eventually the promises and prayers meant nothing either, and I formulated a third attempt.

Avoidance, for me, is a maladaptive coping mechanism characterized by effort to avoid dealing with stressors. The hard part initially was to know what to deal with and what I could deal with at another time without falling back into avoidance. Confronting all my stressors at once is too stressful.

I needed groceries one day because there was nothing in the fridge or pantry. I could go to a restaurant but decided not to, so I went shopping instead. Was that avoidance? Or was it fiscally responsible behavior? My mind constantly performs risk analysis, cognizant of the thousands of horrible things that can happen without warning: the chance of being hit by lightning or a bus, killed by a police officer, or trapped in a random mall shooting. Something could fall on me, or someone could jump out at me. Buildings catch on fire or have planes flown into them; gas lines burst or electrical condensers explode. I formed an opinion about the world as a dangerous place, and I avoided it all to the fullest extent possible.

Now I participate in my life, and I love it. I still feel anxiety but with less frequency or depth. Just a few days ago, I stepped in our garage and raised my hand to push a button to open the garage door. I hesitated because I suddenly felt anxious or nervous about what might be on the other side of the door when it opened. I took a deep breath, pushed the button, and watched the door. Nothing happened.

Three Tips for Avoiding Avoidance

1. Tip of sword. I received this tip from Bobby Bakshi of Resonant Insights. He walked me through an exercise where I imagined of my fears in a cauldron, describing the color, texture, and smell of the liquid. Then I imagined a sword that I could mentally carry with me at all times, and I dipped the tip of the sword in the liquid and discarded the rest. The image is one of a warrior who keeps his fear in front of him by dipping his sword in what he fears, such as the blood of his enemies. I do not avoid what I fear to the extent that it can weigh me down from behind or surprise me, but I keep it where I can see it and use it to motivate me. Use whatever image works for you. The goal here is to see what you fear or want to avoid and cleanly deal with it, like Hercules severing the heads of the Hydra.

2. Riddikulus spell. I find that the *Harry Potter* books can be read as tools to deal with childhood (or adult) fears. This is one of my favorite spells. Imagine what I want to avoid, see it in all of its scariness, and then boldly call out "Riddikulus!" and change it into

something that makes me laugh. J. K. Rowling is correct. Laughter drives the fear away. While I do not believe in the power of wands, I do believe in the power of connecting processes to physical actions. When I use this spell, I move my right arm toward the imagined fear and say the word out loud. If spells are not your thing, try these words from Martin Luther King, Jr: "The words of a motto which a generation ago were commonly found on the wall in the homes of devout persons need to be etched on our hearts: Fear knocked at the door. Faith answered. There was no one there."[63]

3.   Distinguish avoidance from the object. Fear is reasonable if the object of fear is indeed dangerous. I entered a restaurant. The only table available would place me with my back to the door. I started to feel anxious and vulnerable. The fear felt real, but was the potential danger real? I assured myself that a car bomb, or a robbery, or a kidnapping were about as unlikely as getting hit by a meteor. I accepted the seat offered. My anxiety feelings dissipated. In that scenario I judged walking away would create an unhealthy avoidance. On a few occasions, hiking placed me in visible proximity to bears. I experienced similar feelings. Warranted? Yes. Walking away created a healthy avoidance.

Avoiding avoidance can require constant vigilance. How often does someone need to work on this skill? Every time an unhealthy avoidance shows up. Every time. Unhealthy avoidance can feel as safe as healthy avoidance. I do not allow myself to dwell there. Unhealthy avoidance is a stepping-stone on the suicidal path, a security blanket that strangles rather than protects. Whenever you notice yourself engaging in unhealthy avoidance, avoid it. That's healthy.

Accept Help

Some cultures train children to stand up for themselves, often teaching them that it is not okay to ask for help. For most of my life I would help people when asked because I enjoyed helping others. However, if I needed help with my life, I would not ask for it. Funny, isn't it?

Personal coach and friend Caron MacLane once asked me if I needed help. I declined. She responded that she thought I needed help and wondered if I felt uncomfortable asking for it, or did she misread the situation. I pondered a moment, then replied that I could use some help but felt awkward asking. She laughed, helped me, and the problem was solved. I would probably not have broached the subject. But Caron did, which is one of the reasons she is an amazing personal trainer.

Later we talked about this issue. Where else in my life did I need help but wasn't asking for it? Everywhere. Why? Because I had feelings of embarrassment. Why? It was a good question, but I didn't know the answer.

She noted that I frequently helped people when asked. Did I judge them as less than fully human, less than whole, or inadequate? No, I didn't. Then why did I hold myself to a standard that I did not apply to anyone else. Is it okay for others to ask for help but not for me? It was another good question to which I did not have an answer.

She asked if when I helped someone, did I feel good about the experience. I cheerfully responded yes and was glad to get away from haunting questions. Did I imagine that others feel good about themselves when they help people? Again, yes. When someone helped me, did I enjoy collaborating with that person? Another yes. Did I imagine that our world was a better place when people help each other? Four yes answers in a row. It would've been time to go for the closer if this had been a door-to-door sales call.

She then made a comment I still ponder periodically. "Do you see that when you deny others an opportunity to help you, you deny them an opportunity to feel good about themselves? You deny yourself an opportunity to learn and to efficiently solve your problem with someone else. And do you see how you could be denying someone an opportunity to make the world a better place?"

I nodded. I saw that I paid a huge price for my stubborn independence. Still, years later, when struggling with emotions that led to three suicide attempts, I did not ask for help. Funny, isn't it? It was perhaps tragic in my case, although it was understandable for several reasons.

Help is not always helpful. A study monitoring telephone calls to crisis centers found that "15.6% of the calls had at least one characteristic that could be considered unacceptable or below minimal standards of what should be occurring. For example, a small number of helpers told the caller to go ahead and kill himself, were rude or aggressive with the callers, or refused to discuss the callers' problems."[64] I know several suicidals who refuse to call popular help lines because, in their words, the help they receive is no help at all.

Turning to friends, even those one might perceive as empathetic or gracious because of their stated religious views, can result in additional emotional pain and guilt when all you really need is a hug and someone to listen.[65]

Asking for help can create negative consequences. For many years the military rumor mill impressed on soldiers that asking for mental help could result in a discharge, confinement, or assignment to unwanted duties and where they could be constantly monitored. It's odd for a culture that lives and dies by the credos "got your back" or "never leave a fallen comrade." It's also understandable in an organization that places weapons in people's hands and teaches them to kill.

Asking for help feels risky. Ask anyway. Ask until you get the help you need. You need to know what help looks like so that when you receive help you don't need, you can politely say, "That is not the help I need" and move on.

Here is what help looked like for me when I needed it most.

Safety. With three suicide attempts and successful completion of the VA's CPT program, I thought I was done—fixed. I did not need to continue the daily habits that produced the safety, support, and social connections I needed. Several months later, I tumbled into an emotional quagmire. I decided to leave the house for a while and uttered some words to my wife that concerned her. I drove off rather than answering her questions. I realized that I was still capable of ending my life, that my emotional state in that moment would quickly lead me to implement one of my many suicide options. I also knew I needed to be safe from myself. I checked into the emergency room at the VA hospital. I never again wanted to hear myself say the words "I'm not safe," but that was my truth in that moment. I felt embarrassed and ashamed, and yet I was also convinced that I did the right thing. I spent the night in a padded, monitored room. The following morning, I developed a new safety plan with the counselor on call, including renewing medications, daily mental practices, and another CPT refresher training.

Safety for you, your loved ones, and your community is one of your highest priorities. Develop a safety plan. Give copies of it to people you trust, people you can turn to and say, "I am not safe." They should be people who will help implement what works for you. I do not see this step as optional. Your personal suicide solution needs to include a safety plan, and key people need a copy of it. Then you need the courage to admit the truth when you have any thoughts of harming yourself or anyone else.

Medication. For most of my life, the only time I visited doctors of any kind was when I was unconscious or too weak to fight off the people who said, "You need to see a doctor." I felt the same way or more strongly about medications. Medications often do not address the cause, acting merely as symptom managers. But sometimes that is exactly what we need.

Methylphenidate is overprescribed, dumbing down our kids to make them manageable in the classroom. When I was a kid, schools used other forms of discipline. Our children are bombarded with advertising, games and social media and don't get the physical exercise or nutrition they need to properly align their bodies and minds.

Average adults in America are not exactly shining role models of physical and mental health either. I developed judgments, habits, and a lifestyle that, while overtly functional, resulted in deep depression. Just as some people are hardwired to become alcoholics, thus needing to avoid all alcohol, others' psychosomatic systems make them prone to depression or an overabundance of other unhealthy patterns. Depression is a symptom more than a cause. While submerged in depression, I did not take proper care of myself and did not do what I needed to do to break the cycle. Sertraline helped me break free.

I am not advocating medicating all suicidals so that they do not commit suicide. It does not solve the issues, in my opinion, unless the issues are drug company profits, a psychiatric profession wanting to prove itself as a real medical community by dispensing drugs, or family members wanting to create a docile individual because they don't have time to deal with the issues. Yes, I admit I have many judgments about drugs.

I also know how much this particular drug helped me. Many suicidals I talk with voice judgments that are similar to mine. I get it. Even so, please consider medication. I started with 100 mg per day, then dropped to 50, and then stopped. Going off the first time lasted about two weeks. I resumed for a month and then went off again. In the meantime, I worked on getting the right kind of exercise and nutrition to naturally produce the proper physical chemistry. At the time of this writing I am not currently taking any antidepressants, and I feel good about myself. I am also thankful for the medication because it helped me get to this point.

Professional help. I also have a surfeit of judgment around the subject of counseling. Some people are proud to see a shrink. Sometimes I wonder whether they intend their frequent references to their psychiatrist to give the impression that they are the type of people with the time and money to spend on psychiatric services, just as some people wear designer labels. I am not a fan of Freudian psychology, paying someone to listen to me when no one else in my life will. They offer unnecessary solutions to the issues and advise patients to come back next week. This is not what I mean by counsel.

We do not solve problems at the level of the problem. While every problem contains within it the seed of its own solution, we can find ourselves so mired in the muck that we need help to break free. A few days ago I drove past a truck with its front tire in a ditch. Two other trucks stopped to offer assistance. If a truck is stuck in a ditch, someone stopping by with two tickets to a show that evening or someone admonishing the driver for speeding or someone offering the pulling power of a 1985 Yugo GV are not what the driver needs.

Suicide awareness and suicide prevention classes did not work for me. Well-intentioned friends did not work for me. MH doctors proposing only drug treatments did not work for me. Cognitive behavior therapy did. I defined *working for me* as helping me get back on the road of life and giving me the tools and resources I needed to manage my affairs.

Counselors can help. Find what works for you, listen to them, and follow their advice. Do the work. If you don't know how or believe you can't do the work, tell them, so they know how to help you. They can help you read your own mind, but they are not mind-readers.

Veterans Affairs. The VA offers help for veterans. Some veterans are reluctant to visit the VA for help, as I was for a few years. I had no interest in an organization that was part of the system responsible for some of my issues. That might not be rational, but it made sense to me at the time. Not all treatment providers at the VA are veterans. That fact is a block to some. Regardless, I encourage veterans to reach out to the VA. I found the staff at the Seattle VA to be professional, helpful, and unconditionally supportive. The Intensive Outpatient Therapy program at the VA encompasses all three therapies mentioned below. One small act—possibly a phone call—can save a life.[66]

Acceptance Compassion Therapy. The core conception in ACT is that psychological suffering occurs at the juncture between human language, cognition, and direct human experience. ACT is especially helpful for suicidals dealing with shame. For a more complete description of ACT or to find an ACT therapist, research the Association for Contextual Behavioral Scientists.[67]

Cognitive Behavior Therapy. Cognitive therapy teaches people to interrupt and modify thoughts that precede emotions. Behavior therapy looks at how one's environment can reward unwanted behavior. CBT combines cognitive and behavior therapies into a fluid program. CBT is especially helpful for suicidals dealing with depression. The Association for Behavioral and Cognitive Therapies posts a good resource for finding a CBT therapist.[68]

Dialectical Behavior Therapy. DBT combines skill training in mindfulness, distress tolerance, interpersonal effectiveness, and emotion regulation. DBT is especially helpful for chronic suicidals and those with borderline personality disorder. Behavioral Tech, LLC, founded by Dr. Marsha Linehan, who developed DBT, includes a resource to find a DBT therapist.[69]

Leave the Past in the Past

It's easier said than done. Our minds can bring us into the past or bring the past to us within milliseconds of a triggering event. This phenomenon is not easily changed. What we *can* control is our reaction to finding ourselves reliving past events. Some of us spend so much time in the past our futures don't stand a chance.

My past often haunted me and influenced me to accept as true and final an unhealthy version of myself. I decided I could not do something based on whether I had ever done it, or tried and failed. I am not sure how we, as human beings, come to believe this about ourselves. We start life not knowing how to do anything. We can't even feed ourselves or clean up our own messes. If babies bought into the concept that their pasts predict their futures, no one would ever learn anything or attempt anything for the first time or grow from mistakes. Yet, somehow I determined that because I acted a certain way in the past, I would do so in the future. Would I always act irrationally, feel depressed, make inappropriate comments, or turn people away merely by exposing my personality? I thought so, but it turns out that the future is still under construction. I can change.

I used two techniques to break free from the past. The first is one I developed myself. I say out loud the phrase "In the past I may have _____, but from this day forward, I am _____." I repeat it until I feel its power. Fill in the lines with whatever you wish. In the past I may have been shy, but from this day forward, I am gregarious. In the past I may have unintentionally insulted people, but from this day forward, I genuinely compliment people.

When you utter the words, sense how much you believe what you said. If you do not believe it, repeat the phrase until you believe it. If the words you choose are not working for you, change them to what you know is true. If you doubt that your previous actions were unintentional, for example, then drop that word. The key is not in the words themselves but in your confidence that you are indeed on a new path. Any success, no matter how small, will work. Focus on that success as evidence for your new traits.

At one time in my life, I looked at how gregarious people acted. I acted that way, and I too became one of the actors. It didn't feel real. However, when I acted that way, other people started to see me as gregarious, and eventually I started to believe it about myself. Many people today do not believe that I was ever as shy as I claim.

In the past I may have attempted suicide, but from this day forward, I take care of my mental health. This does not mean I will never again feel depressed, or feel that life doesn't contain enough value for me to remain interested in staying on this planet. It does mean that I care for my mental health; if I feel depressed, I will spend no mental energy on worrying I might end my life just because I did so in the past. Instead, I will take care of my mental health.

This second technique is one I learned from others. Write down what you want to leave in the past, and then leave it as tangible evidence of this concept. Some people burn what they write and keep the ashes. I met someone who wrapped each incident, judgment, or memory on a different scrap of paper and then wrapped each piece of writing around a stone. She then placed all the stones in an old travel bag. This physically reminded her of the emotional weight she carried with her. When she thought, *you are incapable of changing,* (one of her beliefs she released), she would think about the suitcase and remember that she left that belief in the past. I know people who symbolically cast their pasts into the depths of the ocean. If it resurfaced, they added some weight to it and let it sink.

At the time of this writing I am on a plane, traveling home from a convention. In the row behind me is one of my favorite sports figures, Russell Wilson, Bose headphone covering his ears, fingers interacting with his phone. I am fortunate to have at least said a few words of greeting, although my wife wishes I had pressed for an autograph. This flight is a mere three weeks after the Seahawk's 2015 Super Bowl loss to the Patriots. Although the Seahawks built a 10-point lead at the end of the third quarter, they lost 28 to24. The most talked-about play of the game was the intercepted short pass into the end zone; many people wondered why the Seahawks didn't call a run play. I observed that Russell Wilson is not continuing to lament or blame others for that play execution or the play call. He is focused on next season. Can the team learn from that experience? Sure. Do the players dwell on it to the point that it prevents them from playing again? Of course not.

Obviously so, one might say. Yet too often in our own lives we relive mistakes, dwell on the emotions of those experiences, and allow the pain to stop us from fully living in the present. The key is to do what we expect our children and our superstars to do: learn from mistakes and then leave them in the past. If something triggers a memory of the mistake, we need to remind ourselves of what we learned, express gratitude for learning such a valuable lesson, and move forward.

Begin Today with a Blank Slate

In the late seventeenth century, philosopher John Locke maintained that the human mind at birth is a complete but receptive blank slate (scraped tablet or *tabula rasa*) upon which experience imprints knowledge. He wrote, "Let us then suppose the mind to be, as we say, white paper void of all characters, without any ideas. How comes it to be furnished? Whence comes it by that vast store which the busy and boundless fancy of man has painted on it with an almost endless variety? Whence has it all the materials of reason and knowledge? To this I answer, in one word, from EXPERIENCE."[70]

We now know that a newborn's mind is not a blank slate. Children are born hardwired with a personality, recognizing certain sounds and acting on preferences.

Similarly, I realize that each day is not exactly a blank slate. Each day carries with it a momentum from the past toward repeating habits, connecting with people we like, avoiding experiences we don't, and keeping a calendar perhaps prefilled with obligatory appointments made in the past. Still, I find benefit in thinking of each day as a blank slate on which I can create my intentions.

What do I want to do today? These appointments on my calendar, do I want to keep them? I might be inclined to think I must do so, but the truth is I do not. Failure to keep agreements with people might have consequences, but I do not *have to keep* any of my appointments today.

A few years ago, my son-in-law, Ed, called me to announce that he was taking my daughter Melissa to the hospital to welcome my granddaughter, "Princess Evelyn," into the world. I canceled all my appointments for the day. Ordinarily I am not one to cancel appointments, although I am more cautious these days about making commitments with my time. *Yes*, I say to myself, looking at the blank slate in the morning, *I am going to keep these appointments today.*

I choose every aspect of my day. I pick my wife as my partner, choose my children to be my kids for the day, and decide how to fill my free time. Having my partner choose someone else years ago and abandon our children taught me a painful lesson: I do not have to do anything I really don't want to do.

Use a small white board or piece of blank paper each morning. Think about whom you want to be this day, what you want to do, how you will show up in the world. Let go of the thoughts *I have to* and *I should* for a moment. This day is about the day you *want to* create. Take as long as you need. When you can see your day unfolding as you desire, write some notes or doodle some pictures about your day. At the end of the day, see how your day turned out compared to your directions. Take from this any meaning you find, and then wipe the board clean or toss the paper, leaving yourself a blank slate for the following morning.

Create Your New Self

I find that focusing on today works better for me than thinking about the future. I have no idea what the future holds. There are too many unpredictable variables for me to feel that I have any control over my future. The one aspect of my future I do control is who I want to be and how I show up.

Some days I do not know whether I even want to be living one year from now or even tomorrow. But if I am going to be alive I want to be the self of my own design rather than the self I might become buffeted by the winds of change.

Years ago, I read Benjamin Franklin's autobiography. I already admired him for several reasons, and when I read how he reinvented himself, I was even more impressed. I encourage you to read his autobiography to get the full story. Here is some of his advice in a nutshell:

- Pick some traits you want add to your life.[71]
- Pick your own definition of the trait.[72]
- Create a method to track your progress.
- Focus on one trait at a time, whether that time is an hour, day, week or month.
- Be honest with yourself, both about where you did not meet your intentions and where you excel.
- Reward your progress with something that supports your goals.

I used this method to transform shyness into genuine gregariousness and change the habit of believing others knew better how to plan my life into a confidence to create and carry out my own intentions. When I decided to make a daily decision to live rather than die, I looked at some of my traits that led me to believe that the world would be better off without me. One trait I decided to change was what I call being the frustrated idealist.

Altering my ideals did not work for me. I still wanted to live in freedom and peace and be part of a positive solution in the world. Yet I came to believe that everything I did toward those ends was a sham. I allowed myself to be a marionette in a production purporting to create what I wanted. In reality, I was creating only power and money for a mad puppeteer. It created a different kind of frustration and felt like denying my true self—something I did for years and do not want to do again. So I examined why having the ideals or ideas about life I hold created so much frustration. I also looked at people I see as idealists who do not seem to exhibit frustration. One of my favorite character studies is the current Dalai Lama. The few times I heard him speak (never in person, sadly) he did not rant, tirade, or blame.

Although I have not yet had the honor of meeting him, I read his writings and stories about him, looking for the secret of remaining calm in the midst of what I imagined to be troubling events that could have frustrated him: freedom for his beloved Tibet, the weight of leadership for the monks who follow his teachings, the shallowness of a world that will honor him with a Nobel peace prize yet refuse to follow simple teachings that would produce peace.

Sometimes I read his stories out loud to myself, as if he spoke them to me personally, like a loving parent reading to a child at bedtime. This story seemed to be one in which he spoke directly to me:

> Let us imagine that we have a next-door neighbor who for some reason or other does not like us and who is always trying to pick a quarrel or get the better of us. If we let him goad us into feeling resentment and animosity, those feelings will not have the slightest harmful effect on him. But on us they will have an immediate

> effect: they will rob us of our peace of mind. After a while we can think of nothing else. We lose our appetite. Or if we do feel like eating, our food is devoid of any flavor. We have trouble sleeping. If a friend comes over to visit, we cannot shake off our mood, and all we can say to ourselves is: "Why does he have to come and bother me?" Word gets around to our other friends, they are surprised to hear about the change in our character, and that we are no longer good company. People stop coming round, one after another, and soon we have no more visitors. Finally, we are left alone to brood over our gloomy thoughts. We cannot even go out and enjoy the flowers in our garden. Stuck indoors by ourselves, seething with angry, resentful thoughts, disheartened and depressed, our hair starts to turn grey, and we begin to grow old before our time.[73]

This was, word for word, my story. Some commentaries on this story call it an exaggeration. I do not. I was stuck indoors for over two years, brooding over gloomy thoughts, resentful, depressed to the point of attempting to end my life more than once. The only difference in my story is that the graying of my heart did not start with the comments of a neighbor but with myriad experiences that led me to lose faith in myself. I went back in my mind (in some sense, in time itself) to take the path of serenity rather than resentment. It remains one of my most important practices each day. I define serenity as accepting what I cannot change.

Serenity, to me, is not an outward manifestation. It is the inward quality that allows me to respond differently to the neighbor and to give a response of kindness rather than bitterness, resentment, or anger. My goal in acquiring serenity is, in part, to serve as a foundation for kindness and how I want to show up in the world.

Living in your new self takes a daily commitment. Yesterday was not a good day for me in the serenity department. I walked out on a conversation with someone dear to me. It wasn't because of anything she said but because of my level of frustration about different events of the day. I judged walking away to be better than blowing up at someone just because the person happened to be in my vicinity. I have work to do in the areas of serenity and kindness. I present this story to you as an example of how to get started on creating your new self and to let you know it is usually not an instant transformation demanding no further maintenance.

I recommend focusing on traits to strengthen rather than eliminate. Start specifically on your suicidal ideology. What drives you to want to end your life? Analyze your physical, emotional, mental, or spiritual components. The world can be a screwed-up mess. It is not about the world; it is about your reactions to it, reactions that sometimes goad you to want to kill yourself. What traits or characteristics can you strengthen that will overcome or replace those that conspire against you? Define, monitor, repeat, and reinforce them.

Review your traits each year. Drop those that do not seem to be genuinely yours. Maybe in the future you will make it yours; add it then. Also remove any you feel you have mastered to a sufficient level— those that no longer need frequent monitoring. It is okay to add them back to the list another year for a tune-up. Finally, in your review, consider adding new traits that build on ones you have already mastered.

Change Your Image

I once met a near supermodel. I say *near* because the she filled the short time we chatted with self-doubts. She thought her thighs had a quarter inch too much fat, and that was the reason she didn't get the mega-star contracts. I thought she looked amazingly beautiful and told her so. She smiled, but it was the opinions of the clothing designers and fashion consultants that interested her. I do not know what it is like to live in that kind of world. She asked me if I thought liposuction would help. At the time, I attended Loma Linda University, a renowned medical center (although not renowned, as I recall, for cosmetic surgery). I was enrolled in the department of religion and knew nothing about medical procedures. Our chat didn't last much longer, and I never saw her again.

But I did wonder whether or not liposuction could change the way she saw herself: not quite as beautiful as her modelling competition.

In 1960 Dr. Maxwell Maltz wrote *Psycho-Cybernetics*.[74] It was a break-through treatise on the growing field of self-image work, with accounts from his plastic surgery practice. Some of his patients did not change their image of themselves after the surgery they thought would change their lives for the better. Others thrived. Why the difference?

One can work Ben Franklin's advice for years and create a new personality, but if one's self-image doesn't change, little will have been accomplished. Changing self-image is different than adding personality traits and probably more important. Traits are an important component of self-image, but self-image encompasses so much more.

To fully break free of my suicidal ideology (which is the whole purpose of this section), I needed, and continue to need, to monitor my thoughts about myself and transform unhealthy self-image thoughts and beliefs and behaviors into healthy ones.

Low self-esteem can be part of a current problem, a result of other problems, and a problem in itself; it can also be a risk factor for other problems. This short section is actually a huge topic, worthy of further study.

Here is a recent experience in which my self-esteem was part of a current problem:

Situation
I am driving with Barb and our two youngest boys. Attempting to discuss recent behavior issues at home, one of the boys is evasive in his answers and then states things we know are not true about him or his activities. Voices are not escalating, and no one is getting angry at each other, but my frustration rises quickly to a level I do not like. I feel defensive and then unsafe.

Triggers a Core Belief
This kind of conversation leads to irreparable hurt.
I do not know how to deal with this in a healthy way

Negative Self-Evaluations
I am not good at these kinds of conversations.
I get too confrontational in these situations.
I will end up hurting someone I care about.
I told myself not to marry someone with kids.

Unhealthy Behavior
I stop the vehicle in the street and put the transmission
into "Park." I announce that I will find my own way
home, exit the vehicle, and disappear into the crowd.

Unhealthy Emotions
I feel sad, depressed, and angry.

Reinforced Self-Image
I do not know how to deal with this situation in a healthy way.

The core beliefs can be about myself, my community, my world, God, or anything else. Core beliefs about myself are what make up my self-image.

We probably have hundreds of beliefs about ourselves. I do not like the labels of *poor, negative* or *unhealthy self-image* as a single label because self-image is far more complex. I might see myself as capable in some situations and incapable in others. I find that when I judge that I have unhealthy self-esteem, I tend to notice the unhealthy aspects of my self-esteem and overlook the positive or healthy aspects. When I realize that a judgment about an unhealthy thought is just a small part of my self-image, I feel better about myself and express myself in healthier ways with others.

I have a belief about myself that if I ever meet a mad Kodiak grizzly in the wild, I am not capable of defeating it in a fist fight. Suppose someone told me, "That's just negative self-talk, man! Think positive! Think you can do it!" My reaction is likely to be, "Okay, I'll think positively. I am positive you're an idiot, and I am positive I would not win a hand-to-hand combat with an angry Kodiak."

This belief about my limitations in meeting mad Kodiaks has never stopped me from hiking in the woods. I take precautions. One of the precautions is *not* a bear bell. Seriously, do people not remember Pavlov's animal experiments in which ringing a bell indicated a meal? If I focus on a story that says "If I meet a Kodiak, I will die!", and I also believe that a particular behavior such as hiking in Alaska includes a high enough probability of that story becoming reality, then I avoid the behavior.

I love hiking in Alaska and British Columbia. I love bears, including Kodiaks. I respect them. I mean them no harm, and I have never felt harm from them. However, I do know people who see wilderness areas as too dangerous. By the way, if you do venture into bear country, a bell is a good idea.[75]

The key for me is not the actual words, *can* or *can't, will* or *won't,* but whether or not the concept works for me or against me. In the vehicle situation above, my self-image in that moment worked against me. I did not want to leave the vehicle but I felt I would do more harm by staying. I felt bad about it afterward. My leaving reinforced numerous self-concepts I wanted to change.

Key steps to changing self-image:

- Monitor your self-talk. Listen to yourself think for a day or two, the self-talk that filters constantly through your mind. Without judgment, just make a physical record of any positive or negative self-talk phrases about yourself. Then review the record. Acknowledge the positives. Then review the negatives. Do you note comments similar to the following?

    I get nervous talking to people I don't know.
    I'm socially inept, and I hate it!
    I must be really stupid.

I am so fat and ugly.
I'm unimportant.
I'm a loser.
I'm unlovable.
I'm not good enough.
I don't deserve to be in a healthy relationship.

- Pick a few comments to work on. For this exercise, disregard any self-esteem comments along the lines of not being able to defeat grizzles in hand-to-hand combat. Some negatives are healthy. Right now look for the unhealthy ones. I suspect this will be easy because you know which ones they are. Circle them.

- Choose what healthy looks like. As an example, take "I panic when conversations turn into personal attacks based on word definitions." Is it true? Yes, I did that. Do I do it all the time? No. Do I want to make it a permanent part of my self-image, my internal operating procedures? Absolutely not. There is no one right way to phrase a healthy self-image phrase. Play with different phrases; pick one that feels right. You can change it later if something else feels like it will work better for you. In doing my work around this specific situation I adopted the phrase I am capable of changing or ending unhealthy conversations in a healthy way that constructively reinforces relationships.

- Repeat. Write down your healthy self-image phrases. Repeat them at least once a day and any time you notice your self-talk expressing a contrary statement.

Distinguish Moral Injury from Trauma Disorders

Yes, I saw people die. I witnessed explosions, participated in services sending body bags stateside, and dealt with civilian and military deaths.

But my PTSD issues stemmed more from my conclusion that they died in vain than the impact of the trauma itself.

Counselors at the VA did not want or did not know how or were not allowed to talk about the moral components of PTSD. I suspected the latter. Treatment for moral injury requires a different discussion.[76] Fortunately, I found alternatives.

My road to moral injury healing began when Bobby, my dear friend and life coach extraordinaire, recommended Mankind Project New Warrior Training Adventure.[77] During that adventure I started to connect with the anger I carried with me about Iraq. A facilitator recommended I look into attending a Vets Journey Home[78] weekend. VJH is an incredible organization that allows veterans to create a scenario in which they feel trapped in the past and then welcomes them home. I met Vietnam vets who were stuck in a scene of people spitting on them in the airport when they returned. Others from different campaigns could not get a particular memory out of their minds. I struggled all weekend to come up with a scenario. The trauma model didn't fit.

With the loving help of facilitators Gene and Patricia, I created a scene containing three chairs, one each for President Bush, Vice President Cheney, and Secretary of Defense Rumsfeld. For seven minutes I outlined my resentments about Operation Iraqi Freedom and about how we dictated their new government for them rather than allowing them to create their own government. I outlined how we lied to the American people about the context of the war as freedom rather than admit the truth about controlling the politics of oil in the Middle East. After I finished, everyone welcomed me home with unconditional love and acceptance. I needed to process my moral injuries before I could start on my trauma-based issues.

Perhaps I also needed the three suicide attempts that followed the VJH weekend. Moral outrage about democracy and freedom was only a surface issue. As I learned later in CPT therapy, I carried strong guilt about failing to prevent injuries from an attack on someone next to me. PTSD treatment is changing to assist people with moral injuries. The treatment differs significantly from fear-based treatments.

Non-veterans also display moral outrage as part of their suicidal tendencies; it includes judgments about the world and their role in it.

Look for moral injury or outrage as you sort through and solve your issues. How you settle these issues may differ significantly from solutions for other issues. You may need some creativity or perhaps suggestions from people who experienced and resolved similar issues.

Given your moral code what will you do differently? If nothing comes to mind immediately, keep reading and ponder that question for a while. You will find some suggestions toward the end of part three, chapter three.

Lengthen Your Fuses

Has anyone ever told you or have you noticed about yourself that you have a short fuse in certain situations? Do you want to learn to lengthen your fuse or even defuse the situation? Here is a technique I learned in cognitive processing.

How people typically see the progress of their own emotionally charged behavior:

Situation ⟶ Emotion ⟶ Behavior

We might tend to believe that the situation forced us to feel and behave the way we did. You may notice this in people who say "You make me angry!" or "You forced me to hurt you!" Are situations automatic triggers? Or is there something we can do about our emotional and behavioral responses to triggers? The good news is that there is something we can control. People who like to blame other people for their improper behavior will not see this as good news because it sheds light on how they are accountable for their own actions.

Detonating a fuse on a stick of TNT is a good metaphor for this process. A situation occurs—perhaps triggered by an event, a thought, or a belief. This situation leads to an unpleasant emotion. Steeped in that emotion I then behave in counterproductive ways. The goal of this process is to lengthen the fuse, which gives me time to alter my behavior rather than immediately explode.

Situation ⟶ Thought ⟶ Emotion ⟶ Behavior

We now know that the situation does not trigger the emotions directly. Instead, situations trigger thoughts, and the thoughts trigger the emotions. It happens so fast that many of us do not see how our thoughts are involved. We move straight to emotion and then the emotionally charged behavior. Our thoughts playing the role of the fuse explain why some people are triggered by certain situations but not others.

This is a real example I processed about eighteen months ago. I couldn't find something. I distinctly remembered where I left it, but it wasn't there. I became angry that someone would move something of mine without my permission. No one was home, and my anger continued and increased until everyone returned. Barb had moved it to do some cleaning and didn't think to move it back. There was no intention to harm, irritate, or goad. My level of anger, however, I rated at 70 percent on a scale where 100 percent is the angriest I ever felt. My level of anger, as I expressed it, seemed unjustified for the situation.

Why did I feel that level of anger over someone moving something of mine? Did I feel that level of anger anytime something moved or was it just that one item or just that occasion? I quickly realized, in part based on family feedback, that I exhibited anger anytime someone moved something of mine. I analyzed my anger with the following process:

1. **Recognize the key thought.**
   The best time to write down your thoughts is when you feel the emotions rising. In that moment, ask yourself, "What am I thinking?" It probably will be a number of simultaneous thoughts. Write them all down without judgment. Then sift through the thoughts for the one or two that hold the most energy in the moment.

In the scenario above I did not ask myself anything in the moment. The more time that lapses, the more difficult this step becomes because judgments and emotions interfere. The first thought that comes to mind is not always the primary thought at play. I kept working with rephrasing thoughts until I wrote down the following: "I always need to be aware of my stuff, or bad things will happen."

When I wrote that version of my thoughts, immediately a memory of my childhood flooded my vision. I grew up poor, even by the standards of the day. My parents could not afford many purchases beyond utilities and food. They surprised by brother and me one day with used bicycles when I was twelve or thirteen. I was ecstatic! My first bike! I did not care whether it was used. Most of my clothes and toys were used. My brother and I thanked our parents profusely.

On Sunday morning, we set our bikes in front of the garage so that we could ride after lunch. We lived in a rural area with few neighbors, all of whom we knew and trusted. Approaching home, we could see smoke coming from the area of our home—black smoke. It wasn't a huge plume, as if an entire house was on fire, but big enough to see from a mile away. As we pulled into the driveway, we spotted our bikes burning. Someone set our bikes on fire—just our bikes.

I could still feel my emotions from forty years ago: strong anger, both toward someone who would do this and at myself for leaving my stuff out where someone could harm it. My sense of trust changed because I could not imagine it was a random event involving a stray car, which rarely happened. Could someone we know have done this to us? I also sensed fear. If the person burned our bikes, what else would he or she do to our things when we were not around to protect them?

I had not thought of this memory in a long time, yet the emotions from it surfaced as fresh as that Sunday itself. I found the key thought. Will your key thoughts contain the same level of energy or trigger powerful memories? Not necessarily, although they usually contain a level of energy corresponding to the triggered emotion.

2. **Challenge that thought.**
   We can challenge thoughts in several ways:

   - Look for all or nothing phrases that are likely not true.
   - What is the source of the thought? Isis that source reliable?
   - Does the thought confuse high versus low probability?
   - Is the thought out of context—only true in some situations and not others?
   - What is the evidence for and against the thought?
   - Is the thought based on feelings or facts?
   - Is the thought based on irrelevant factors?

Let's look again at the thought I generated above. *I always need to be aware of my stuff, or bad things will happen.* The original source of the story is my own experience, and I trust my memory about that story happening as I recalled it. What I learned from that experience, though, is not correct.

For example, bad things can happen even if I am aware of the location of everything I own. Additionally, I have also experienced times in my life when I was not aware of my stuff's location, and yet nothing bad happened. Both the *always* and the *will* are exaggerations.

The use of exaggerated language changed a factually low probability to a near certainty in my mind. What is the probability that something bad will happen when I am not aware of where all of my stuff is located? Actually, it is not much different from the probability of something bad happening when I *am* aware.

3. **Create an alternative thought.**

Simply recognizing the source of my key triggering thoughts and the inflammatory structure of the language will reduce any thought's potency. To completely diffuse the situation, I recommend also creating a new thought built on the truth as I now see it.

I jotted down two alternative thoughts at the time.

a. Even if I am not aware of my stuff, everything can be okay.
b. I can be on control of my life without needing to be in control of all my stuff.

The second phrase seemed less powerful to me. I questioned why I needed to be in control of my life. The first phrase worked better and is now condensed to the final four words: *Everything can be okay.*

Now, if I can't find something of mine and I am convinced someone else moved it, I simply remind myself that everything can be okay. It's the same trigger but no explosion.

Accept Accountability.

Suicidals often need to rethink the way they hold themselves and others accountable. In the past I often judged myself harshly; I blamed myself, felt guilty, and believed I deserved punishment.

Years ago, I met Bert Reinks, a fireman in southern California. The subject of accountability came up during a group conversation. I stated that I thought of myself as an accountable person. Bert disagreed. There was no blame or shame and no conflict; it was just a matter-of-fact disagreement. He pointed out instances in which I over-promised and under-delivered while blaming circumstances outside my control. He challenged me to be a man of my word.

Accountability is not about blaming or punishing ourselves or others.

It is simply a perspective from which we acknowledge our responsibilities toward outcomes. If I state that by the end of the month I will achieve a certain target and then do not, the unaccountable me blames the economy, the weather, or the lack of opportunity for people like me. The accountable me looks at *my* role. What could I have done differently? Did I do what needed to be done, when it needed to be done, whether I wanted to or not? Was the intent unrealistic? What did I not see or misunderstand?

Accountability is not concerned with fault but rather what it takes to create better results. When I ask myself the preceding questions, the goal is not tally my blame and then flog myself accordingly. Instead, I learn what to do differently and reset my intention.

Until we accept ownership of our actions, we will be helpless to change our results. When we accept that our actions influence outcome, we enable ourselves to create the results we desire.

Accountability shifts our focus from defending ourselves to learning from failures and success. During my almost twenty years in the US Army, a mission or exercise always ended with an accountability meeting, when we discussed the mission in terms of "sustain and improve." What did we do right that we could carry forward to future missions, and what could we improve to make the next mission more successful?

In the past, failure stopped me emotionally. I failed. End of story, nothing else to do, can't change that. I often wallowed in that emotional quagmire even if I was 90 percent successful. Not 100 percent successful? Failure!

Now, failing to fully reach an intention is feedback. Recognize the success and learn from it (sustain). Identify weak points and adjust (improve). This shift in how I view accountability created a mental environment in which I now understand that disparaging circumstances and truculent people need not prohibit me from reaching my goals.

This section challenges you to set some new goals, change your mind or behavior, and even reach out to people who might not work with you in ways you want. If you do not fully succeed in your first attempt, let go of blaming yourself or others. Simply learn and try again. This is the true essence of accountability.

Balance Your Bad Self

The first time someone told me to "go on with your bad self!" I did not know how to respond. I furrowed my face. I'm bad? He laughed. He explained that this phrase indicates *keep going in just that amazing manner.* In this concept "bad" is better than good! The phrase became popular with the B-side song of the same name by Sonny Smith in 1973. If you want a positive attitude adjustment, find a recording of that song, and play it every morning as you plan your day. You will walk taller, smile more, keep your head held high with confidence, and move with purpose.

Personal solutions are, to this point, primarily a mental exercise. Fully healing oneself and creating a healthy balance in life requires a complete human experience solution. As you expand your mental toughness remember to develop your entire self. Some teachers describe the human self as comprised of four primary (inner self) elements: physical, mental, emotional, and spiritual.[79] By expanding yourself externally you can also add occupational, financial, social, and family factors. For now, keep it simple. I don't want you to feel overwhelmed.

If the aspects of your life mentioned below are not currently healthy, success may take time. Just get started. Do something specific every day to advance in each of these areas. Balance yourself daily, and you will live a balanced life. It's simple. You can do it.

1. **Fix your finances.**
   Life is more fun with money. Travel, keep bills paid, give to causes you believe in, and watch the smile on the face of a child with an ice cream cone. Lack of money is one of the more common reasons to commit suicide, although wealthy people also end their own lives. An abundance of money brings with it a different set of problems.

   It turns out that the key to happiness is not money or lack of money but our relationship with it. Do we work hard to pay for a home we don't have time to live in, drive cars that we have not fully paid for, wear clothes to impress people we don't even like? Or does our dance with money bring light into our lives?

Some people strive to get out of debt—a worthy goal. Yet their striving brings more strife. Does getting out of debt or experiencing any financial accomplishment bring happiness to someone who lives without happiness because of a perceived lack of that accomplishment? No, that path to happiness is a gerbil wheel trap. Money is a necessary tool, a way of navigating our world, the one agreed-upon bargaining tool in a system designed to make more of it for those who control access to money.

Play the game, but play it with your own rules. Develop a healthy relationship with money. Have enough of it to spread some around to those in need, starting with yourself. "Neither a miser nor a spendthrift be," as someone wise once wrote. Money is a powerful gateway to a deeper understanding of yourself. Earn justly, spend wisely, and enjoy both.

2. **Pump your physique.**

I am not here to pump you up. You have to do that yourself. Exercise at least three times per week for at least twenty minutes. Better yet, find a way to be active every day. Find something you are comfortable doing and make it fun. Challenge yourself. What you do does not matter as much as doing it. There are no excuses. Your mental health needs a fit body. You know this.

Constructive physical exercise boosts happy chemicals, reduces stress, and improves self-confidence. Some routines work better than others, but any routine works better than none at all. Get started. If you have an exercise program already, keep up the good work. If not, here are tips to get you started.

- Jog, walk, bike, or dance three-to-five times a week for thirty minutes.

- Set small, daily goals, and aim for daily consistency rather than perfect workouts. It's better to walk every day for fifteen to twenty minutes than to wait until the weekend for a three-hour fitness marathon. Frequency is important.
- Create exercises that are fun or enjoyable. Some people prefer classes and group activities. I prefer solo pursuits.
- Exercise to audiobooks, podcasts, or music. Many people find it's more fun to exercise while listening to something they enjoy.
- Recruit an "exercise buddy." It's often easier to stick to your exercise routine when you have to stay committed to a friend, partner, or colleague.

Be patient with yourself when you start a new exercise program. If you are currently sedentary, you may require about four-to-eight weeks to feel coordinated and sufficiently in shape so that exercise feels easier. Keep going.

3. **Sooth your spirit.**
Our spiritual self is our connection with the universe. It defines our core foundation, purpose, identity, and our very reason for living. Some suicide workers believe all suicide is, at its root, a spiritual issue. The spiritual self turns intention into reality and creates something beautiful and useful out of detached components. A salubrious spiritual self is a magician, a miracle worker. It permeates all that we think, do, say, and experience.

Express yourself through music, art, or writing. Dismiss any thoughts of *not good enough*. The intention here is the expression itself. Keep this to yourself if you want, although eventually you will want to share your expressions with others you carefully select.

Spend time alone in a location that feels peaceful to you, one that reminds you of everything that is right about the world. Reflect on that vision of the person, community, or world you want to create. Then stop thinking and just listen. Ask what is mine to do and wait for an answer. This is the secret of all spiritual masters.

Special Thoughts for Young Adults

Some people believe that part of us chose our parents before our birth or that we at least chose to come to this planet in human form. I do not believe either of these ideas. We may, however, choose to leave. I recommend you don't, although I understand why you might want to. I did. We see a huge spike in suicide around age fifteen, although thoughts of suicide start much younger.[80]

Kids and young adults recognize truth and honesty in more ways than we credit them. Older adults can act as if we all buy in to the lies we regularly tell ourselves to help cope with the world we've created. Young adults find themselves surrounded by phonies and hypocrites who say they believe one thing but act differently. You see adults praised in public, yet if everyone knew what happened behind closed doors, the praise would perhaps turn to scorn. The instability of their house of cards is as obvious to you as the nudity of an emperor parading around in what his public relations' team refers to as "new clothes."

Adults tell you to play life by their rules, and the number-one rule is to play it safe. Don't rock the boat, stir the pot, or disturb the balance. These same adults also tell you that you live in the land of the free and home of the brave, while they exhibit neither freedom nor courage. Yet they wonder why you don't believe their stories or acquiesce to the game they play.

You are not the first person to be confused, irritated, or frightened by human behavior. You do not need to participate in a contorted, psychologically imprisoned world. You may walk an alternative path of your own choosing. The life you want to live is waiting for you. Use your time to work on yourself, building the best self you know how to create. You will probably always want to have a community of people, so also work on your community-building skills. Also, young adults can impact larger communities and even nations. Perhaps *Oh, the Places You'll Go*[81] was written just for you. I recommend the hardcover version (rather than the e-book) for two reasons; the hardcover portrays the pictures better, and you can start amazing conversations when people see you reading the hardcover book. Some people think this is a kid's book. Little do they know.

Your goal is to care for your entire self, physically, emotionally, mentally, and spiritually. Understand what you need; it can differ from what you want. You might believe that you don't control your life enough to give yourself what you need. I encourage you not to dismiss your capabilities. Many people of all ages discover that once they set their intentions, events and circumstances shift in unforeseen ways.

Consider your physiological needs: food, shelter, clothing, and those needs without which you cannot function successfully. Make these your first priority. Perhaps others already supply you with everything you need. Remember to thank them. Use wisely the time others require to create basic sustenance. When I was ten, my dad told me it was time for me to start earning money if I wanted new clothes. I don't recognize that level of poverty today in the US Northwest where the basic needs of so many young adults I meet is determined by whether or not they are keeping up with the latest music or electronics or fashion trends.

Here are two tips about your needs, if I may. Attracting more into your life works better when you are grateful for what's already shown up. Second, you may receive support for your needs from unexpected sources. Say yes. In my youth I turned away support, thinking I needed to do everything on my own.

Next, work on your safety. How can you keep yourself safe in healthy ways? Healthy solutions do not harm yourself or others. Look for results based on calm contentment rather than fear. Some people believe there is safety in numbers, although I find I require a certain level of trust before additional people help me feel safer. Others believe in the safety of personal weapons. Weapons can also make you a target and can be used against you. If you are going to carry a weapon, learn how to use if confidently and effectively to defend yourself. If your circumstances are not safe, reach out. Keep looking. Ask. Prod. Perhaps a safe house or some kind of temporary shelter is available nearby.

According to Maslow's hierarchy of needs, the next level of the pyramid is love and belonging. We'll touch on that in the next chapter.

Summary

This is not a chapter to merely read and set aside. Creating the life you want takes effort. Start with changing yourself. This work is only as difficult as you make it. If you hold the intention that the results will come to you with ease, they shall. Work smart rather than hard. Feel free to remain with this chapter for a while. You do not need to work on the community building solutions until you are ready.

Read this summary list slowly, and rate yourself. Where are you already strong? Which ones need immediate attention?

Avoid Avoidance   Accept Help
Leave the Past in the Past   Start Today with a Blank Slate
Create Your New Self   Change Your Image
Lengthen Your Fuses   Accept Accountability

These skills can transform your life from one so burdened that you want to end it to one encompassing enough joy that you chose to stick around for a while. You are the change you waited for. You are your own suicide solution. Now is the time.

CHAPTER 2

COMMUNITY SOLUTIONS

"And man needs a feeling of achievement. We all do. We've got to be able to be recognized for doing something well. And somebody's got to point it out to us. Somebody has got to come up occasionally and pat us on the shoulder and say, 'Wow! That's good. I really like that.' It would be a miracle if we could let people know what was right rather than always pointing out what is wrong."[82]

"Mental health experts say high-profile, public suicides like this one are rare and troubling, because they often receive media coverage that can glamorize self-destructive behavior and lead to copycat deaths.

'The next vulnerable person thinks this is a good option. It's a very real safety concern,' said Misty Vaughan Allen, State Suicide Prevention Coordinator for the Nevada Division of Public and Behavioral Health.

She said what happened in this case is unusual. Only about one-third of people who kill themselves leave behind so much as a note, let alone send notice to the media.

From what she has read so far about Noble's death, it clearly was not impulsive, Vaughan Allen said. 'It looks like we as a community missed some opportunities to help this individual.'[183]

Creating a social network for a suicidal requires only two ingredients; the suicidal and other people. Sometimes putting just these two ingredients together gets complicated. In my youth I did not know how to talk to people. Oddly enough, I did not mind speaking to groups. Groups didn't talk back. Carrying on a conversation with a stranger? Just put a gun in my hand, and let me end the horror. But then that is in part the reason for this book. It is possible to learn social skills. I spent years studying body language, gestures, public speaking, and conversations. Some people consider me an expert, but often I still feel out of place in public.

We all have social networks. Perhaps there won't be enough close friends to carry our caskets at our funerals, but we meet and need people on a daily basis. At a grocery store we might use a self-checkout and never talk to a single person, yet the simple act of buying groceries for two weeks requires the cooperation of thousands of other people: store owners to invest their capital, employees to stock shelves and clean floors, truck drivers to carry goods, ship personnel to bring produce or other goods from overseas, growers, processors, and inspectors. I am not at all suggesting that you get to know all these people. I am suggesting that we suicidals are not the self-sustained, isolated islands we imagine ourselves to be.

This section is divided into three sections. The first is for suicidals who are determined to commit suicide and want to lessen the impact on their community. The second is for suicidals who want to build a strong, supportive community rather than commit suicide (again, perhaps). The third is for people who want to support a suicidal but experience resistance.

Bracing Your Community if You Are Going to Commit Suicide

I appreciate research studies crafted with objective definitions, isolated variables, and measurable results. I am not aware of any studies on lessening the impact of suicide on one's community. Ethics boards, and society in general, would reject a study designed to allocate people who want to commit suicide into two groups: one that includes these hypothetically impact-lessening variables and the other that does not. "You want to commit suicide? Yes, you qualify for this study. Now, do you want to commit suicide in a way that lessens the impact on people who know you? Or do you want to maximize their trauma?" Such a study is a horrible idea![84] If we theorize about such a study, though, what factors might separate the two groups?

To Maximize Negative Impact

- Total surprise, no advance warning
- As gruesome a death as possible
- A statement found afterward blaming specific people
- Public death and blame, e.g., create a news event that a news team would cover and then shock the world

To Minimize the Impact

- Tell close community members in advance.
- Let them know you love them.
- Let them know it is not their fault.
- Let them know why you want to end your life.
- Let them know you are not asking for their permission or agreement or help.
- Disclose approximately when, where, and how, only if they will not interfere.

I know several other ways to maximize a negative impact because I spent too many hours of my life contemplating that subject. However, I do not actually want to help suicidals accomplish that intention. I do want to help suicidals think through the potential effect of their actions and what they can do to potentially minimize that impact if they choose.

I strongly believe that total surprise and lack of communication increase the negative reactions to suicide. It happens every time. Based on that evidence, can we determine that communicating about the suicide will lessen the impact? For example, if it is true that a lack of communication (which might be objectively defined as knowing whether the suicidal intended to carry out such an act) leads to a significantly negative emotional experience for the survivors, can we therefore conclusively argue that good communication about the decision will produce less wounding affects? No, we cannot.

Demonstrating that *If A, then B* is true, does not prove *If not A, then not B*. To deduce the latter from the former is what a philosophy or rhetoric professor might call the "propositional fallacy of denying the antecedent." Here's a simple example.

My dog is a Goldendoodle. Stated in rhetoric fashion, if it is my dog, then it is a Goldendoodle. This statement is true. However, it is not true to state "If it is not my dog, then it is not a Goldendoodle." Goldendoodles are one of the most popular breeds in America today. Two of my friends own them, one from the same breeder. No, the antecedent is not necessarily true. The antecedent *could* be true. Lots of dogs are not Goldendoodles. We just do not know whether a particular antecedent is true based only on the truth of the primary statement.

What about the frequently toted connection between mental illness and suicide? One psychiatrist states on her website that "Suicide is NOT normal" (caps in original). She cites an American Foundation for Suicide Prevention statistic that 90 percent of all people who die by suicide have a diagnosable psychiatric disorder. She believes psychiatric disorders are treatable; therefore, suicide is preventable if people seek treatment. Her conclusion is a fallacious[85] and professionally self-serving argument. Psychiatry is not the solution to suicide she claims.

I am not a psychiatrist, a psychologist or a researcher. I am a suicidal with formal training in critical thinking. Questions such has what do we know and how do we know it have life and death repercussions in this complicated field that is rife with faulty reasoning, poisonous guilt, and insufficient answers. There are many important questions but few proven answers.

I wish I could point to solid data that telling your community in advance about your suicide will lessen the emotional impact. There isn't any, other than my belief that it is the right thing to do with the people you care about. It might also have negative consequences, including them interfering with your intention. Telling people that you want to end your life can sometimes change your community as much as a failed attempt. You might find yourself involuntarily confined and unable to follow through. Providing advance warning can be self-defeating.

Prepare yourself for the discussion by thoroughly understanding your reasons why. You will be asked. Can you articulate your reasons clearly and succinctly? Think through all the details and their potential impact. Your choice of how you will end your life will itself amplify or diminish emotional trauma. Pick a peaceful rather than violent method. Your timing is relevant. Do not choose family holidays or special occasions such as birthdays. Ask not so much for their support as how you can support them. This is neither an easy nor fun discussion.

Will you be alone? Will someone accidentally find you later? Stumbling across a dead body is traumatic; when that dead body is someone you love, it is exponentially traumatic. What will you look like? Peaceful or mangled and messy? Perhaps you choose not to be found—one of my favorite suicide fantasies. But no body often leads to lack of closure; it is sometimes an emotional torment more horrible or longer lasting than a messy ending.

If suicidals want to decrease or minimize the negative impact of their suicides on people they care about, the best approach is to discuss the topic with them. I also believe such a discussion is not for everyone. If this discussion could result in additional harm, then proceed carefully. I do know that when I am depressed, I think differently and see the world through a depressed lens. For example, I judge or perceive people as less friendly. It is too easy for someone who is depressed to decide such a conversation will not help.

Your suicide will emotionally harm people you care about. Are you going to show them you care by addressing these issues in advance? Or will you just leave them a useless note? I urge you to initiate the conversation, even if with only one person. Start with someone you trust. This may be the hardest yet most rewarding conversation of both your lives.

This section is about the negative impact suicide creates for communities of the suicidal. Suicide's reverberations can devastate a social network and sometimes include fatal results. I want to speak directly to suicidals right now. I wish I could look into your eyes. Your suicide will emotionally, psychologically, and spiritually harm people you care about and who care about you. Since you care and because you care, before you end your life, let them know this is about you and not about them. Please. You might find, like I did, that you no longer have the same motivation to die. Or you might decide to follow through with your decision. At least you will die knowing that they know the real reasons for your action.

Prior to my fourth suicide attempt, made while writing this book, I did not tell anyone of my plan. A few key crisis-level supporters could read the signs. I lied to them about my level of safety. I was not safe. They did not specifically ask if I was safe, and they did not ask if I had a plan. I now know these are key questions to ask. If they had, I am positive they would have known whether or not I told them the truth. Why didn't I tell them, even though I had already written the previous paragraphs telling others to do so? I judged that none of them would agree. I picked their opinions for them without checking in.

The reason I am telling you this is because several of them told me how news of my suicide would have impacted them. One theme kept surfacing. Part of what hurt the most is that I didn't talk to them about my issues.

My brother Pete visited me during my confinement. I told him, "This isn't about you."

He replied, "The hell it isn't!" I look at him, a bit stunned. I had not heard that tone from him before. I looked in his eyes. I expected anger, but I saw pain and deep hurt.

"I thought we had a relationship where we could tell each other anything. You were at my house last night. And you told me you were okay. You lied to me! This is also about me, Frank! It's about us and our relationship."

He was right. My suicide was not just about pain; it was also about the way I decided to leave. It was about every person who cared about me. I was not honest with them. As Caron MacLane told me two years ago, I denied them an opportunity to help me, to work together to find a solution, to sympathize, and to hold me in their thoughts or prayers. Maybe, after all of the discussions, they would have supported my decision to die. Then we could have found a more peaceful ending for all of us. But I denied them that.

I hope suicidals will find in this book inspiration, encouragement, and maybe even a reason to live. If there is one thought I implore you to comprehend and act upon, it is this: *before you activate a plan to end your life, talk to at least three people who care about you.* Don't let them find out from the police or the news or a phone call from a grief-stricken family member.

Framing Your Community Discussion

Your suicide is not up for a vote. You decided, and you are going to follow through with as little negative impact as possible. Your purpose in the discussion is not if others agree; they might not. You are not asking for their permission or their help. They will likely offer neither. Do I *know* that this will help reduce any of the tsunami aftermath? No, but I strongly believe it.

Take away their sense of blame by telling them your personal reasons. Teach them that it is not a reaction to anything they have done but a proactive decision on your part to end your life on your terms. Help eliminate secrecy by giving them permission to share your story. Or perhaps share your story yourself.

Reduce potential ostracizing by giving them a story of courage they can share when people ask. Ending life on one's own terms is an act of courage, not cowardice. Your social network can continue to hold its head high within the network.

Most importantly, leaving a legacy of proactive self-determination creates some positive ripples in the loss they will inevitably feel. In such moments of sorrow, they can also remember that, even in dying, you thought of their well-being.

While research may not yet know if this strategy works, I have seen it work a few times. A recent example is Brittany Maynard.[86] What if every decision to end one's life could inspire courage, love, and compassion toward our survivors the way Brittany's did? It should not take a terminal illness of a gifted younger adult to bring about a healthier closure. Perhaps anyone contemplating suicide who takes the steps mentioned above can help his or her social network avoid unhealthy repercussions.

Rebuilding Community after a Suicide Attempt

On July 24, 2015, I decided to end my life. I sent emails to close family and friends to say good-bye; I also sent a few to tidy up some details about my business and then purchased a shotgun. Initially I did not know the location, as long as it was remote. While I finished the emails and texts, replies started flooding in. My phone started ringing. Within minutes more than a dozen people wanted to talk to me about my decision. I ignored all their calls. But given the wonders of modern communication, I could not so easily ignore the texts and email summaries my phone automatically screened. They reminded me of how much I meant to them and how much they would miss me or need me. They sent pictures of precious memories. One of my daughters sent a picture of my granddaughter. She asked what I wanted her to tell Princess Evelyn about why grandpa wasn't going to see her again. That one came close to engaging my heart, but my steel-cold intention ignored it.

Another aspect of modern communication is how easily, under the right circumstances, authorities can trace a phone. I noticed a system alert that my phone had been "found." A veteran with a weapon, suicidal intentions, and a known disdain for the military—last pinged near a military base—would certainly start people looking. That is when

I turned it off and headed an hour away to my final destination, the Tahoma National Cemetery.

I walked into the cemetery close to midnight. It was partly cloudy, and dim moonlight illuminated the tombstones. Tahoma encompasses more than 150 acres and is the final resting place of over 23,000 veterans. I walked to a secluded area near the center, a spot where police cars with search lights would never find me. I didn't want to be found for a while. If the shot didn't instantly kill me, the blood loss would. Then I encountered a support group I had not previously considered.

My mind started thinking about the body bags we sent home from Iraq. Some of those warriors were buried in this place. I thought of Vietnam vets, Korean vets, World War II vets, and other campaign veterans. Opened in 1993, Tahoma is a newer cemetery, so only KIAs from campaigns since then are buried there. Some may have died later, as a result of injuries sustained in combat. Some died by their own hands. Many continued to love their lives after service, passing away in the myriad ways that overcome us all. Tahoma's motto is "Where Heroes Rest."

I loaded the shotgun, ensured the safety was off, placed the end in my mouth at an angle my research revealed would work best, and placed my thumb on the trigger. Then I started to see them. They weren't ghosts exactly, not in a way anyone else present would see. They appeared to be shades, ethereal beings, moonlit shadows of the past assembled to witness my entrance into their world. Then a question came: "We will witness your death, as you have witnessed others. But first we want to know, what are you dying for?" I told them about my physical injuries, my emotional maelstrom, and my anger at our federal government. They listened and waited.

Surrounded by the great cloud of witnesses, I could not pull the trigger. Had I earned the right to enter this rest? Yes. But my story and my struggles sounded hollow compared to the stories I told myself about them. Part of me screamed to pull the trigger. I had said my good-byes. The plan had worked perfectly so far. If I backed out now, I would potentially face criminal charges for my actions. I would face my support group, whose members I said good-bye to and ignored. I would need to restart my business and face bills I could not afford to pay. I raised my weapon again. They watched and waited. Three times I positioned myself to pull the trigger. The third time I set the weapon down I pushed the safety button and unloaded the cartridge. I would not die this way. I vowed instead to live my life as they had lived theirs—giving life everything I had until the very end.

I walked out of the cemetery, found one house in the neighborhood where someone was returning home, and asked to use the phone. Then I waited for the police to arrive. I had locked my keys in the car on purpose. Driving home was not an option. Besides, I would rather face the police at the cemetery, away from family.

After intense questioning, an officer asked me to sit in the back of a squad car. An ambulance arrived to take me to a hospital with a secure emergency room and a psychiatrist on staff at that hour. Per protocol they strapped me to a gurney. Twenty minutes later, they checked me into a monitored room in a secure area of the hospital.

About a dozen members of my support group came to the hospital, some of them having already driven to a spot near the military base. The doctor allowed a couple of them to visit. Together we developed an action plan. A few hours later, released and facing no criminal charges, I walked into the lobby to face my support group.

Given that this was my second visit to such an emergency room, the doctor was initially inclined to send me to a state facility. Why didn't she? It became obvious to her that I would be more closely monitored—in a healthy way—by my support network than a state facility could ever do. In the lobby we hugged, cried, and even laughed. We comforted each other. I promised each of them I would never put them through such an ordeal again. I intend to do the work necessary to make that promise a reality, no matter how long I live.

Someone remarked later about the scene in the waiting area during the hours I remained inside. There was no blame or accusations toward each other or about me, just unconditional love the entire night. This is the ultimate expression of a healthy social network. The ultimate benefit, though, is tapping into one's network early so that one doesn't need this expression in a hospital waiting room.

Benefits of a Healthy Social Network

Healthy social networks add special meaning to life. You are welcome to create as many social networks as you want, networks as small as only one person, peer support groups, or large networks that include family, tribes, or connections around social causes or political issues. Communities help us share good times and overcome difficult ones. Communities can help improve our mood. Happiness is contagious; smiles float from one face to another spreading their charm.

Social networks help us reach our goals. Whether we are recovering from PTSD,[87] giving up alcohol or tobacco, or otherwise improving our lives, encouragement from a friend can boost our willpower and increase our chances of success. Networks help us cope with stress and depression.

Communities can boost immune systems, reduce the type of isolation that is a major contributing factor to depression, increase happiness, and add value to our lives and the lives of people we care about.

On a trip to the Grand Canyon West Cultural Center, my wife and I chatted with an elder from the Hualapai tribe about the recent suicide of a young tribal man—a sad, growing trend among his generation. Family and elders involved in his daily life were not enough. Also in current news is the rise of suicide among the younger generation of the Lakota tribe at Pine Ridge.[88] I am not a tribal member, yet my heart aches when it hears such stories.

Social networks did not and could not stop me from my three suicide attempts. However, they did help me recover and gave me reasons every day to stay on my life path. Creating social connections is a vital component in suicide recovery. In my past I did not know how to create healthy social networks. I missed opportunities when people reached out to me, coming across as disinterested, even when I felt empty inside. The benefits are real; the personal gains are worth every effort. If someone as true a social misfit as I am can create healthy communities, I know anyone can do it.

Build Your Network on a 3G Foundation

Grace. I blasted someone once for a mistake she made, focusing on the negative impact it made on my life. She asked me for some grace. That stopped me cold. I ranted about something in the past we couldn't change and made her wrong in the present. I apologized. Grace does not mean we let people do whatever they want to us; grace simply means extending mercy, even if we believe the recipient has done nothing to deserve it.

I also needed to extend grace to myself. I would not tolerate from others the mental lashings I gave myself. I judged myself so harshly that I felt I did not deserve to live, as if I could restore some measure of honor to myself through hari-kari. We can see grace at work in the world if we look for it. Let us extend it to ourselves and those around us. I envision the pastor for the church of my youth extending his arms toward the congregation and saying, "Grace to you, and peace from God our Father." Use grace on a daily basis, and you will begin to see that you deserve a life filled with joy.

Gratitude. I now wake up every morning filled with gratitude rather than dread. In suicidal throes I am not grateful for much. It's hard to leap from deep despair to boundless gratitude, at least for me. If you can make the transition quickly and easily, I encourage you to do so. I needed to practice gratitude, build up this trait as one strengthens muscle. To build gratitude, simply find something to be grateful for in every aspect of your life, and focus on those aspects.

Gratitude is the opposite of finding fault. In the past I thought, *I could be grateful for my house if I lived there, but I will not be grateful for the house I do live in."* My house provided a roof over my head, warmth on a cold night, shelter in a storm, and a gathering place for my family. Yet when I focused only on its detriments or how it was not as nice as other people's homes, I was not grateful for the blessings it added. My home was not the only thing I found wanting rather than counting the blessings it or someone else added to my life.

What we focus on we attract and get more of. Do you want to add to your life more of the things for which you can be grateful? Start expressing gratitude for what you already have. I enjoy living in gratitude rather than fear, anxiety, and criticism. I rarely now have the previously constant thoughts that my life sucks, and I should end it. I still experience fear, dread, and remorse but not as deeply or frequently.

Giving. It seems counterintuitive, but one of the universal principles to acquiring more of anything—money, love, friendship—is to give some of it away. How do we create community? We create it by daily doing something nice for someone we don't know and doing it with no expectation of reciprocation. Give smiles away. Say thank you. I am practicing making eye contact with people and smiling when I thank them. I find that they smile back and accept my gratitude with all the sincerity with which it is intended. Yes, after years of working on my social skills, I still look for ways to improve them.

Give compliments. Don't practice flattery; that won't build strong communities. However, a sincere compliment can lead to continued dialogue and deeper friendships. I complimented someone recently on his shoes, and he talked with me more in the next fifteen minutes than he had in months of previous occasional greetings at business meetings.

I also give people permission. I sometimes hear people lament that they "shouldn't" do something that is good for them or they want to do, such as ask for a raise or take a vacation. They listen to some voice in their head telling them no—often a parent who is not even in their lives any longer. So I tell them, "You have my permission to do that." Yes, I have said this to strangers. It works!

Become Trustworthy[89]

I initially titled this section "Rebuild Trust." Then I listened to a TEDTalk by Baroness Onora O'Neill in which she argues that we cannot build something that is a gift from someone else. Trust is the gel that holds social networks together. However, people instinctively find it hard to deeply trust suicidals. They might love us unconditionally, listen to us when we need to vent, yet hesitate to trust us if they know about our suicidal ideations. We sense this, which is partly why we find it hard to discuss our suicidal thoughts. We want people to trust us, and we don't want to disappoint them. Often we do not see that the decision to remain silent is itself the first step in eroding what we want to protect.

If people emotionally invest in us, we become friends and share experiences. While looking forward to more of the same, they know at any moment we might rip this happiness out of their lives. So they naturally distance themselves to protect themselves from the pain of possibly losing a friend to suicide. As long as the threat of suicide exists, we cannot create the friendships and social networks we crave. The solution is to take the suicide threat out of the equation in a way they can trust.

The goal here is not as much to convince people they can trust you but to become a trustworthy person and build your social network out of the people who trust you. What I see as the first step differs from most articles and books on this subject. We need to start with trusting ourselves.

Find a mirror. Look into your eyes. Hopefully, at this point, you are smiling at yourself. If not, that's okay; it's just a sign that there might be something to work on. Tap into your intuition, the part of you that senses whether or not something is true. Hold your eye contact. Now say this statement out loud to yourself: "I trust myself." Are you convinced?

During my years of depression or PTSD or whatever label people used, I judged myself as untrustworthy. I thought, *People shouldn't trust me because I will eventually hurt them. My friends and the world would be better off without me.* Does this sound familiar? While I find this thought pattern common in suicidals, each one arrived at this judgmental space by traveling a unique path.

A few seconds before the IED exploded, my intuition told me we were about to be hit. I have no idea how it knew. Some people call intuition the voice of God, since it often tells us things we cannot possibly know. Others call it collective consciousness, while others acknowledge it but without explanation. We all have it. Intuition is part of the human experience. I didn't often hear it up to that point. But when I did, it was right and conveyed information that was of tremendous value to me or someone I cared about.

"We're about to be hit," my intuition warned. All my senses became fully activated beyond the already heightened levels of a solo HMMWV traveling in northern Iraq. My eyes darted everywhere, and my mind quickly processed anything out of the norm. The gunner was in position, the blast windows were closed, and I tightened my grip on my M16 with these observations: the tracker looked normal, the other soldiers were following protocols, a lone figure was on a bridge ahead in front of a vehicle with the hood up. He was not looking into the engine compartment; he was watching our vehicle. I saw the shopping cart on the side of the road with something in it; the driver started to quickly change lanes, as we are trained to do, and then the explosion happened. Black smoke, tires blown, steam coming from engine area, hydraulic fluid spraying the windshield, captain yelling into the radio.

The other back seat passenger and I got the gunner inside. He was screaming and bleeding, much of his upper body damaged with shrapnel, half of his face damaged. The captain was already on the radio asking for the nearest place we could meet a helicopter. Thank God, the vehicle was still moving, even though all four tires were blown and damage to the engine compartment was spewing dark liquid on the windshield.

I did not know it at the time, but in the aftermath of that experience I started to doubt my intuition. Why would it tell me about danger if there was nothing we could do? Then the judgments kicked in. Maybe I failed. Maybe my intuition spoke to give me an opportunity to hit the swing's release switch before the explosion and save the gunner.[90] I started to believe I could not be trusted to know what to do in a tough situation. I compounded that by deciding that others shouldn't trust me. They might get hurt. I couldn't protect them.

Regaining trust in ourselves can take time, forgiveness, and patience. The process works better when we have a few people in our lives who trust us and hold a vision of us as trustworthy, people with whom we can share our fears and be honest about our intentions. When they ask us if we feel safe, we can tell the truth. Honesty about our intentions and emotions is one of the most important actions we can take to increase trustworthiness.

"How are you doing, Frank?"

"I feel sad."

"At least your emotions match your expression. [Smile] What are you sad about?"

"I don't know."

"Anything I can do to help?"

"Nothing comes to mind."

"Are you safe?"

"Yes."

"When you discover what you are sad about, will you check in with me?"

"Sure."

I have had dozens of such conversations. Sometimes I don't know why I feel sad or depressed or despondent. If I promise to check in with someone, I do. If I do not feel safe, I tell the person. People can only help us to the extent we remain honest with them.

Do not force or manipulate anyone to extend trust to you. You can only control your own actions and thoughts. Become a trustworthy person, and build a support team of people willing to trust you.

Find Your Team

Some people deal with high stress by smoking or overindulging in alcohol, drugs, sexual exploitation, gambling, or a plethora of other behaviors a normal society defines as unhealthy. They can also participate in these behaviors recreationally. Suicide is in a unique category. A suicidal doesn't wake up the morning after a suicide feeling sick or used or abused. Done right, he or she does not wake up.

When is the right time to build a support network? Today and every day. It's that important. At the time of my previous suicide attempt four and a half years ago, there was one person I considered to be on my team, and her intervention saved my life. During the most recent attempt, dozens of people rallied into action. I knew most of them previously; they were family members with whom I did not share my feelings. Finding a team is more about social interaction skills than it is about finding the right people.

Relationships ebb and flow. One friend of mine categorizes relationships as people who come into our life for a reason, for a season, or for a lifetime. When we hold a clear vision, as she does, for the why of relationships, we can create healthier expectations and boundaries. Here are a few categories of reasons why people can join your team:

Crisis. These are network members who agree that you can call them 24/7 in case of an emergency. You know their contact numbers. These names and numbers are on a card you can access at any time. They are on a card you carry in your wallet or are listed as favorites on your phone. I suggest you also have one or two crisis line phone numbers ready just in case you can't reach any of them during a crisis. Suicide.org posts crisis line numbers for every state in the US and some international numbers.[91] I recommend you find a couple of local numbers on your state listing rather than the national hotline. Call them. Let them know that you are building a support network you can call during a crisis and ask what support they offer if you call them. If their level of support works for you, add them to your emergency call list.

Talk-walks. There is something magical about walking and talking that does not happen during phone calls. These walks are not for crisis times; their purpose is to talk about your frustrations and ask for feedback or support about how you are handling situations. This is not about blaming or shaming others, and it's not about a tale of woe or reinforcing a victim mentality. The people you walk with should help you focus on your own plan of action. This is also a verification for them, a check-in so that they can see how well you are (or are not) doing. These walks can be mutually beneficial in that you can also offer the same support for them.

Checking in. Phone, email, video links, messaging, letters, forums, blogs. We can instantly check in with people all over the world. So why don't we? Two days before my most recent attempt would have been the perfect time to check in with any of the several people I promised to call when in that emotional space. It didn't seem like a crisis at the time; I didn't need crisis intervention. But deciding to not check in morphed into a crisis within forty-eight hours, and then it was too late. I now have a written document that gives several criteria for checking in and a signed promise by me that I will do so.

Healthy fun. Get to know some fun people, people who can make you laugh, people who inspire you to smile more about yourself and the world. Seek out several names for this list. The more the merrier. Such people are usually socially active, so don't get discouraged if they don't drop everything to spend an evening with you. This isn't a crisis list. It's just about hanging out and having fun, so find ways to have fun together. Consider sponsoring a group event. There was a time in my life when I lost interest in most healthy activities. It's okay to be in that space temporarily, but you don't want to stay there.

Coach Your Team

Loving someone enough to support him or her through a suicide crisis does not automatically make someone a good support team member. One way to open a person's eyes to the broad scope of suicide awareness and prevention is to ask the person to accompany you to a class or support group. However, to fully support you, the person needs to know your specific triggers and distress signs. They won't learn that in a class. You need to tell the person the truth. If you do not know all your specific triggers and distress signs, then work through the personal solutions chapter again (and again). Also consider professional help. I find DBT particularly helpful for chronic suicidals in this regard.

For specific support around triggers I use three categories: daily maintenance, warning signs, and crisis. The idea is that some people are better skilled at supporting you during different phases of distress. In the daily maintenance phase, you may need help with medications, exercise, healthy eating, hygiene, laughter, or spiritual rituals. When distress increases and your warning signs are present, you may need counseling, increased frequency or intensity of certain daily activities, and people who can help you stay aware of the fullness of your life and avoid making rash decisions. When you are in crisis, you need team members who know how (and are not hesitant) to engage in crisis intervention. This may be talking you through a crisis point, calling 911 or a crisis line, or taking you to an emergency room. Some people may be good at all three, but if they are only good in one category, keep them on that expansion team. We need all the support we can get.

Support Your Team

Ideally your network of people, those who will encourage you when you need help to get through a tough spot, will consist of three-to-five people. A one-person social network is not always physically or emotionally available. While it is not necessary that your support team work together or even know each other, they can help each other better help you with a little collaboration from you.

Staying up all night on a suicide watch is mentally, physically, emotionally, and spiritually exhausting. Dropping everything to listen to you because you feel suicidal is a significant commitment. Listening to you rant about your same issues, while seeming to make no progress toward resolution, drains people's energies. They need support as much as you do, and part of that support needs to come from you.

Thank them. Talk to them when you are doing well, when you do not need their help, and remember to thank them for their support. Mention both what they did that helped and the difference it made in your life. "Sofia, thank you for listening to me vent the other night. Your smile and attentiveness helped me feel unconditionally supported. I found myself focused at work the next day, and that coworker didn't get under my skin."

I once sent a beautiful note card with the same handwritten expression to several friends. A few days later I crossed paths with one of them; she told me that she appreciated the card so much that she told a mutual friend about it, who informed her that he also received one with the same sentiment written inside. She continued to describe how her delight diminished when she realized that what seemed like a private message was sent to several other people. Thank you cards are fine, but make them personal. Thank you calls and personal chats are even better.

Appreciate your support team. I do not recommend giving someone a gift just because you think you must. A sincere *thank you* will mean more to your support network than a gift given out of compulsion. However, you can impact the lives of your team members in a meaningful way by solving a problem for them or giving them a gift that means something to them. Listen attentively and observe. A friend once mentioned a favorite brand that he could not find when moved to the area. I located a source for him a few blocks from his new residence. Sometimes what means the most to people is just spending time with them while they perform necessary but unpleasant tasks, going for a walk, or offering to watch their kid(s) or pet(s), so they can have some time to themselves. What they give or do for others is often a reflection of what they find meaningful.

Reach out whenever necessary. Change what you are able. You can become more capable at both of these than you currently believe.

Tips on Working with Your Team

Practice *I* statements. Communicate what you feel, think, need, and want. Don't make assumptions about other people, including your support person. Support is not a gossip session. Avoid using the words *you* or *we* unless they are specifically appropriate. For example, "I feel humiliated," rather than "You humiliate me."

Practice confidentiality. Confidentiality is not just for your support team about your issues; it is also about anything they may say about their own issues in supporting you. Support will disappear immediately and turn into conflict if you break confidentiality.

Stay clear with all support people present. If you are not listening to their support because you have a charge against them, have the courage to bring it up first to clear it out of the way. In a recent group meeting, someone stopped the conversation and mentioned that he could not focus on the discussion because someone said something to him that really bothered him. That someone was me. I did not know him well and did not know his struggles; I made an innocent remark in comedic fashion (as I often do and need to monitor such remarks) that deeply bothered him. We cleared it up, and he understood I had no malice toward him. Both the relationship and the group dynamic were strengthened because he stated his truth in that moment. Staying clear is immensely important; it is not a skill people acquire easily. The process or procedure is not as important as the intention. If both you and your support person want to maintain a clear relationship, then you will make it work.

Supporting a Suicidal

There is no TV reality show more draining or rewarding than actually supporting a suicidal. This responsibility is not for everyone. We do it because we love the person and because perhaps we've been there, and we know what it's like to live in scary, dark spaces. We also see a vision for humanity as a caring community that's often different from the world we see the moment we walk out our front door.

The World Health Organization reports that over 800,000 people die from suicide every year.[92] Some people who have attempted suicide or work with suicidals believe that none of these people wanted to end their lives, that suicide or suicidal ideology is always a cry for help. I do not agree with this. Most suicidals, at some level, desire to end their lives. Many of them are also conflicted about this desire, since they may also feel compulsions that compete with or counteract that desire.

Have you ever wanted to both eat chocolate cake and not eat chocolate cake at the same time? There are feelings of being conflicted, divergent, torn by a tension we don't know how to resolve, and a deep, overwhelming anguish. Suicide is a real choice; sometimes it genuinely looks like the best or only option available.

Support in its simplest form is providing help in whatever part of a suicidal's life you are willing to be involved with. Many suicidals often do not know what to do or how to ask for help. Reading the previous section may spur ideas. Help them help you help them. Do they need support for daily maintenance activities? What symptoms show up as a crisis builds? What works for them to mitigate that crisis? What items on their support needs list are you willing to provide?

Support Posture

Take all suicidal comments seriously. A few days before my planned suicide in Iraq, our unit participated in mandatory suicide prevention training. On my way into the training session I remarked to our first sergeant that if I had to sit through one more prevention training, I might kill myself. He scowled, as first sergeants do, and replied in a hushed tone, "I know what you mean." Mine was unquestionably a suicidal comment, a comment made by someone with an existing plan to commit suicide. Was it a cry for help? Absolutely not. In fact, if he had shown any concern, such as asking if I had any intention of harming myself, I would have smiled and apologized for a bad joke. Yes, we should take all suicide comments seriously.

But what exactly does that mean? Does it mean if someone makes a comment that we anonymously call 911? I don't recommend that choice for several reasons. However, consider adopting this strategy. If someone—anyone—makes what could be considered a suicidal comment, reply, "May I ask you something?"

If the person consents, proceed with, "I lost a dear friend to suicide. I take all suicide comments seriously. This won't go beyond me, but I do want to ask. Do you have any plans to harm yourself or others?" Carefully observe facial expressions and body language.

Leave mental illness diagnoses to the professionals. Don't dismiss suicidal comments or gestures by thinking *That's just their depression/ mood disorder/schizophrenia talking.*" Whether it is or is not, they're dead if they follow through with their plans. Unless you are a trained professional and they are coming to you for treatment, don't treat them like mental health patients. Treat them like people who need your help getting through a tough spot. Seeing suicidals as whole and complete can often mean so much and may mean giving them hope enough to continue. Listen rather than diagnose.

Consider confinement. Involuntary treatment is not your decision. However, I strongly recommend you know how to access such treatment in your area before you need it. Involuntary treatment should be a last resort and limited to instances where persons pose a serious risk of physical harm to themselves or others in the near future. (Defining confinement criteria is a topic we will revisit in the national policy section.) Where I live, designated mental health professionals evaluate people with mental disorders for possible involuntary detention in psychiatric facilities. Under our state laws people can be detained in specified facilities for up to seventy-two hours without their consent and for an additional fourteen days with a court order. This service is accessed 24/7 by calling a local number or 911 or visiting emergency rooms of certain hospitals.[93]

Be yourself. Just offer what you are capable of doing. Help suicidals create a large support network so that they are better supported and not fully dependent on you alone. You don't want to be burned out in your efforts to support them when they need you the most. Use your own language. The words you say are less important than how you say them. Let your love and concern shine through your words and actions. If you have strong emotional or judgmental reactions to their situation, set them aside in full confidence that you can process them later. For now, focus on helping them through their crisis. Try to remain calm and accepting, nonjudgmental and sympathetic.

Maintain proper boundaries. Controlling people with suicide threats is a manipulative and destructive game. "If you leave me, I'll kill myself" is a cry for help but not a reasonable request for support. You do not need to live your life on their terms. Suicidals issuing demands or ultimatums to you is a good indicator that you are not the best person to help them. It's not that you can't or are not able to do so; it's just that they will not hear messages from you in a way that will benefit them. Remain firm in your boundaries, goals, and intentions. Communicate clearly. Help them find the help they need. My experience is that you can do everything suicidals ask, and they may still end their lives because it really isn't about your behavior. Their issues are much deeper.

Create your own support. It takes a lot of chutzpah to help a suicidal. Witnessing a loved one dealing with thoughts about ending his or her life can stir up many difficult emotions. Remember also to take care of yourself. Find someone you trust to talk to about your feelings and experiences, someone who will help you stay on task. Lead by example. Be willing to seek out the help you counsel your suicidal to accept.

Let go. It is not your responsibility to make your suicidal healthy. You can offer support, but you can't get better for the person. He or she has to make a personal commitment to recovery. Suicidals need to take their own necessary medications, perform their own exercise routines, and honestly face their own demons. Support may be your responsibility, if you chose to accept it, but getting well is theirs. Let go of anything that is not yours to do. Yes, it's scary. Let go, if for no other reason than to set an example for your suicidal so that when their wellness requires them to let go, you can show them how.

Know the Warning Signs

A suicidal might not connect with you and say, "I am having suicide thoughts. Can I talk to you?" Sometimes you need to initiate the conversation after noticing warning signs. I considered myself a master of disguising warning signs or suicide plans. However, there is no way that changing from an attitude of living life to deciding to die can remain totally invisible. When working with a specific suicidal, the best plan focuses on specific triggers and warning signs. Until you get to that point, here are some general warning signs to consider:

- A sudden sense of calm or complacency after being extremely depressed. Although this can be a sign of recovery, it can also indicate a decision to commit suicide.
- Phrases such as *I wish I hadn't been born*; or *I'd be better off dead.*
- Seeking access to guns, pills, knives, or other objects that could be used in a suicide attempt
- Unusual focus on death or dying
- Writing poems or stories about death or dying
- Feelings of helplessness or hopelessness
- Feeling trapped, as if there's no way out
- Belief that things will never get better or change
- Feelings of worthlessness, guilt, shame, and self-hatred
- Feeling like a burden ("Everyone would be better off without me.")
- Giving away prized possessions
- Making arrangements for family members
- Saying good-bye, as if the person expects not to see you again
- Unusual or unexpected visits or calls to family and friends
- Withdrawing from others
- Increasing social isolation
- Desire to be left alone
- Self-destructive behavior
- Increased alcohol or drug use

- Reckless behaviors such as aggressive driving
- Taking unnecessary risks

I frequently like to be left alone to isolate. That, in and of itself, does not mean I am thinking of harming myself. After my first suicide attempt, my partner at the time started to treat me as if even one warning sign meant a need for immediate crisis intervention. I get that. I came close to turning her world inside out. She felt scared and worried it might happen again; she didn't know the best way to help me or herself. She had trusted me but lost that sense of trust. However, always jumping right to crisis mode didn't work for me. I felt she didn't understand. I decided to become better at disguising warning signs rather than open up to her about my feelings. We created an unhealthy paradigm about warning signs.

How many suicide signs indicate a crisis? The mental health profession typically views a diagnosis as a certain number (or higher) of a set of signs or symptoms. For example, DSM-IV Criteria for a Major Depressive Episode states, "Five (or more) of the following symptoms have been present during the same two-week period and represent a change from previous functioning; at least one of the symptoms is either (1) depressed mood or (2) loss of interest or pleasure."[94] Less than five means we do not categorize that mindset or time spent in those symptoms as a major depressive episode. Such labels can be useful for helping mental health patients and can be mandatory for insurance carriers before covering treatment. However, when it comes to suicide, my former partner was right: it only takes one. So how do we gauge the appropriate response level, given that a suicidal might not agree he or she needs intervention?

Ascertaining Risk Level

Here is the best method I know. Someone is at the greatest risk for suicide during a combination of specific intention, means, and a time goal; a suicidal is thinking *I will end my life at 8 o'clock p.m. on Thursday by*— The more specific the goal, the less likely the suicidal is to talk about it, but the more likely warning signs will appear. When you see any warning signs that concern you, ask the following questions without condescension, using a nonjudgmental, matter-of-fact approach:

Plan
- Do you have a plan, or have you been planning to end your life?
- How would you do it?
- Where would you do it?

Intention
- Do you intend to commit suicide?
- Have you ever thought things would be better if you were dead?
- Have you ever thought about killing yourself?

Means
- Do you have the (drugs, gun, rope) that you would use?
- (If yes) Where is it right now?
- (If no) How will you get it?

Time
- Do you know when you would do it?
- Do you have a timeline in mind for ending your life?
- Is there something (an event) that would trigger the plan?

Based on the answers to your questions, mentally categorize the person's risk level. If you are uncertain, choose the most serious one that fits.

Low: Some suicidal thoughts. No suicide plan or access to means. Says he or she won't commit suicide.

Moderate: General suicidal thoughts. Vague plan or means that are not lethal. Says he or she considered or might commit suicide.

Crisis: Specific suicidal thoughts. Specific plan and means that are lethal. Says he or she will commit suicide.

For a more detailed explanation of this concept from a professional clinician's viewpoint see this helpful resource from the Suicide Prevention Resource Center (SPRC).[95]

Crisis-level Intervention

Do not leave someone alone in a crisis. Get the person help. If you cannot think of a better response, call 911 or a hotline. You don't want to add any more triggers at this time. Questions such as "Who can I call right now?" work better than asking for permission such as "May I?" The person might not give permission, and it is not a good time for a debate.

More than once, as a suicidal, I have been asked to voluntarily cooperate in a crisis moment, knowing that I would voluntarily do what the police or MH doctor on call at the hospital asked, or I would do it under restraint. I choose voluntary, but not everyone makes that same decision. Hopefully your role will be to get the person some professional help rather than be the one to restrain him or her.

If suicidals have access to means they will use, consider confiscating those means if possible. Do not ask them to retrieve lethal means such as weapons. Ask them where it is located and have them accompany you while you retrieve it, or keep them away from the area and let the professionals handle that part. You do not want them holding those means in their hands during a crisis. If they will not cooperate, don't argue with them; note the means and location and acquire later while keeping them away from that location in the meantime.

How do we know when a crisis moment is over? When is it safe to leave suicidals alone? Sometimes one person's intervention, which can be as simple as listening to them and letting them know you care, is enough to downgrade a crisis. If you know them well enough and are comfortable considering the crisis over without a second opinion, then move on. However, some people will tell you they misjudged situations and regretted it for the rest of their lives. I recommend not downgrading a crisis without corroboration.

If a suicidal completed a safety or crisis plan that has been reviewed by his or her mental health professional, and if, under the terms of that plan, I can clearly tell that the crisis has passed, then I would likely determine that crisis intervention was no longer needed. However, if the MH professional has not reviewed the intervention plan or it does not contain a specific section for "how to know when I am better," then I would not take the suicidal's word for it that the crisis is over.

Suicidal crisis intervention is similar to CPR and EMS training wherein personnel are taught to continue CPR until relieved, until the victim regains spontaneous pulse and respiration, until the rescuer is exhausted and unable to perform CPR effectively, or a more qualified medical professional determines that assistance is no longer needed. We could rewrite the CPR policy as a suicidal crisis intervention protocol for psychological first aid (suddenly envisioning a national nonprofit created to coordinate a nationwide training program similar to CPR and emergency first aid, SCIs carrying wallet sized ID cards with this oath on the back). Suicide intervention is considerably more complicated than CPR, but these steps are the same. Continue SCI until the crisis clears or relief by another SCI or appropriate professional arrives.

Someone walked into a group meeting looking exhausted. I asked, "How are you?" He smiled. "Good, tired. On watch all night." He relieved someone else watching a mutual friend, and then another friend relieved him. One of that suicidal's friends stayed with him, awake and on guard, until the crisis subsided. Sometimes that is what it takes.

As SCIs we are surrounded by an abundance of support including 24/7 access to 911 and numerous hotlines. Rather than continuing one physical action until we are no longer able to do so, we can coordinate any necessary support. Might we stay awake with someone until we are exhausted and need to sleep? Possibly, like the guy mentioned above, but it's rare. Exhaustion more frequently happens, as it did to my friends and family, from staying up all night at the hospital, waiting for word from the doctors on my condition.

In one sentence, suicide crisis intervention is getting suicidals the help they need, when they need it, and whether or not they want it.

Non-crisis-level Support

My non-crisis support helps me create a life for myself that is so full of joy, laughter, safety, and peace that crisis-level suicidal thoughts never develop. If, in the valleys of life's ebbs and flows, I find myself moving into moderate risk, I remind myself that I am capable of creating the life I want. I did not always believe myself capable. When warning signs appeared in the past, I sometimes felt trapped and judged that I had not truly changed. I criticized myself for once again entombing myself. Now, I note the presence of risk signs as one might notice the weather report before deciding how to dress for the day, or noting a cold symptom and deciding to take zinc or vitamin C. Judgment, panic, and fear are replaced with compassion, support, and awareness. Creating this way of living took time and the support of many people who believed in me—often more than I believed in myself.

Specific support might look different for each suicidal. What works for me might not work for someone else. For example, a medication that helps me might harm someone else. Music that helps me become centered can be different from what helps someone else remain calm. I shared a few songs from my emergency playlist with a suicidal; they were soft melodies with easy-to-understand, positive lyrics. He played a few of his songs for me, all heavy rock, which makes me feel more distant and isolated. Your most precious contribution to suicidals may be something only you can bring, possibly helping them see themselves as the amazing beings you know they are.

General, non-crisis-level support we can implement for any suicidal is a multifaceted prism that produces beautiful light in the world, as unpretentious as letting your inner light shine.

Smile. Many suicidals comment on how cold people seem. Yes, part of this perception is depression interpreting their environment for them. Still, even a depressed person warms up to a genuine smile. According to Dr. Jerome Motto, a psychiatrist from UCSF, a suicidal left a note simply stating, "I'm going to walk to the bridge. If one person smiles at me on the way, I won't jump."[96] He jumped. Since then, bridge workers and many locals consciously smile at people walking along the bridge. The world needs more smiles.

Listen. Listening without passing judgment saves lives. Many suicidals divert their plans based on simply a phone call, a caring person on the other end of the phone who is simply listening to their stories. Active listening, coupled with a genuine smile, may be all your suicidal needs to avoid a crisis. Ongoing listening might help suicidals remain well below crisis level. If you are particularly good at listening, numerous crisis support centers could use your help.[97]

Encourage professional help. Encourage your suicidal to see a mental health professional. You can also help locate a treatment facility or take them to an appointment. Call a crisis line for advice and referrals if necessary. Do everything in your power to help your suicidal get needed help. But remain encouraging. Crossing over into nagging or badgering can escalate issues.

Make a safety plan. A safety plan sheet I use is included at the back of the book. Creating a safety plan for suicidals is part of most professional services, so perhaps you just need to ask for a copy. If they cannot produce one, or, as in my case, the safety plan does not work for them because they just treated it as an exercise to get the doctor off their backs, create one with them. Include elements of a safety plan that can help them help themselves identify any triggers that may lead to a suicidal crisis; it should include steps to mitigate each of those triggers and contact numbers for any doctor, therapist, or friends who will help in an emergency.

Stay involved. *Call Me Maybe* might be a fun music video, but it does not work well with suicidals who believe they can't be helped or they are just an intrusion. Proactively offer assistance. Stop by, invite them out, have fun, and create a better world together. Involvement is more than just checking in to make sure they take medications. You don't want to create a scenario where they dread seeing you. Help them see the beauty they bring into the world. If they develop a solid sense of purpose and reasons to live, their risks of returning to crisis level decrease significantly.

Community on the Suicide Spectrum

In the Personal Solutions section, I introduced the concept of a Suicide Spectrum:

$$\longleftarrow \hspace{8cm} \longrightarrow$$

−10 (Suicide) (Life) +10

Simply stated, your non-crisis role, as someone supporting suicidals, is to help them look in the +10 direction of their lives and take a step. No dragging, pushing, or pulling, just walking alongside. Help them realize that −10 emotions do not need to lead to a −10 thought, and a −10 thought does not need to lead to −10 behaviors. In the midst of a strong negative experience we can still decide to move in the direction of life.

When the kicking and screaming is over, when the anger subsides, when the fear stops, that is the time to help your suicidal create a new paradigm, a new story.

Ask your suicidal, "What is a + thing we can do right now?"

If the person cannot think of one, list off several + activities that helped in the past. If you have a copy of the person's crisis planning sheet, read off the activities listed as potentially helpful, and see if any resonate in the moment. Remain patient yet firm; create a + behavior of any magnitude before you leave them alone.

Teach this powerful technique to other community members, and help your suicidal learn to create this pattern as a response to any (–) situation. In time, your suicidal can generate this pattern on his or her own; when that happens, life can begin on a new, magnificent trajectory.

Your community has its own collective score on this scale. What can you all do together to move your community toward +10? The easiest way is to reconfigure your community to exclude anyone suicidal and others like them and add only positive, upbeat people. What if we accepted as our mission in life the goal of helping everyone in our community move in the same direction to a +10 life? I strongly believe your community, including your suicidal, will accomplish more working together on this goal than if your suicidal is the only focus.

Your suicidal might not thank you, at least not to the extent you deserve. Supporting a suicidal is something to do for love, not for praise. Even so, I want you to know that I recognize your effort and that supporting a suicidal is one of the most emotionally, spiritually, intellectually, and sometimes even physically demanding roles a human being can take on. I appreciate your efforts to help your suicidal and how all our communities and world benefit from your work. God bless you.

CHAPTER 3
NATIONAL SOLUTIONS

The goal of saving lives can only be achieved by a combination of efforts at multiple levels. States, territories, tribes, and communities can play an important role in implementing suicide prevention programs that can meet the needs of diverse groups. In doing so, it is important to involve multiple partners, including agencies and organizations involved in public health, behavioral health, injury prevention, and other areas.[98]

A physician helped her dying mother end her own life following repeated and explicit requests for euthanasia. The physician eventually received a short, suspended sentence. While the court upheld that she did commit murder, it offered an opening for regulating euthanasia by acknowledging that a physician does not always have to keep a patient alive against his or her will when faced with pointless suffering. As the first euthanasia test case, it broke social taboos in a country with strong Christian traditions. It also reflected a wave of awareness among many young medical professionals about the limits of medical care and patients' self-determination.[99]

In 2001 the U.S. Surgeon General's office published its first *National Strategy for Suicide Prevention* [hereafter referred to as the *Strategy*]. In his preface, then Surgeon General Dr. David Satcher wrote, "The [*Strategy*] is not the Surgeon General's strategy or the Federal government's strategy; rather, it is the strategy of the American people for improving their health and well-being through the prevention of suicide."[100] The *Strategy's* forward chronicled suicide prevention efforts up to that time and is worth reading for anyone interested in the movement's history.

I appreciate the combined effort of numerous organizations and believe the *Strategy* did represent the best of what we knew about suicide at the time. However, we now know mental disorders are far more complex. For example, objective 3.2 from the 2001 *Strategy* states, "increase the proportion of the public that views mental disorders as real illnesses that respond to specific treatments."

One does not cure or render ineffective a suicide thought that produces mental disorder simply by prescribing a medication in the way one might use antibiotics to combat a bacterial infection. Even with a treatment program and community support in place and a suicidal appearing to follow all its components, someone can still choose suicide, and everyone is stunned. Why? The way we think about suicide is incorrect; it is not fully formed.

The surgeon general's office revisited its *Strategy* and published an updated version in 2012. The recent *Strategy* paints a more realistic picture about suicide. Suicide prevention shifts from a mental health issue to a broader health perspective, so that "a person who is struggling with depression and thoughts of suicide is given the services and support he or she needs to recover from these challenges and regain a sense of complete physical, mental, emotional, and spiritual health and well-being."[101] The 2012 *Strategy* includes a table mapping all the 2001 *Strategy* objectives into their 2012 counterparts, if applicable. The former objective 3.2 now "focuses on promoting the understanding that recovery from mental and substance use disorders is possible."

While the 2012 *Strategy* shifts the focus into objectives more likely to reduce suicide, as of the end of 2015, suicides continue to increase. I want to influence the way we think about suicide. How we currently frame the discussion is part of the problem. I also want to propose a few ways individual suicidals can participate in the national discussion. It could give them a reason to live and possibly detract from them ever thinking of suicide again.

National Solutions

Empower Individuals. I recommend that we expand the theme of empowering individuals to recognize that individuals are already empowered to end their own lives. The federal government did not give us this power, and it can't take it away. We, as individuals, know we own this power. Suicide is sometimes not the tragic conclusion of a confused or unstable person but the conscious choice of a rational mind, seeing no better solution to issues or stressors.

One of the stressors mentioned is loss of a job. I agree with this assessment. Does the federal government contribute in any way to people feeling like they are painted into a corner? Not that it owns up to in this strategy. Consider working harder and longer hours, until April twenty-fourth of this year, solely to earn the amount of taxes demanded by the government, taken by force if necessary, by one of the most aggressive collection agencies in the world. Or consider the stress of daily listening to our own government divide into groups and manipulate us, as if to create a diversion to keep us from noticing the decreasing level of personal freedom or autonomy in favor of increased federal powers about our daily decisions. I could continue but hope this is enough to state the point.

I realize that this *Strategy* is the creation of the surgeon general's office, an office respected by the American people, if that can be said of any government agency these days. It does not set fiscal policy, and it does not pass regulations. And I am truly grateful for this *Strategy* and all those who collaborated in its creation. Still, I do not feel or believe the surgeon general's office is on my side.

This is what I hear this theme saying to me as a suicidal:

We don't want you to end your life. Why not? Well, if you are a productive member of the workforce, you add income and payroll tax into our coffers. We want your money. The higher the suicide numbers the more citizens complain to us to do something, and we don't like to have to listen to our citizens. It's best that they just do what we tell them and leave us to do what we want. When we attend international forums, other countries with lower numbers treat us as if we don't have control over our population, and that is embarrassing.

No, these are not exact quotations, but the *Strategy* does allude to each of these ideas. It's just my interpretation, the irrational thoughts of someone who is so crazy he attempted to take his own life. Perhaps, but if I am the person you are trying to reach with this strategy, I want you to revisit the empowerment theme and really mean it next time. Empower me. Show me options. Give me the authority to live my own life, including ending it on my own terms. Convince me you are on my side.

Or, do you have a different goal for individuals, one not mentioned in this *Strategy?* Do you really want free citizens, living independent lives, and an empowered, self-determined, educated populace? Providing a government for such people is significantly more difficult and time-consuming than governing a placated population. What if the surgeon general's office could be used to more fully control people through the use of drugs?

Rather than manipulate religion as the opiate of the masses, what if we could convince a significant number of people to voluntarily take medications that will increase their happiness, make them more compliant, and allow the government to control more of their lives with less complaining? If I were the surgeon general assigned with such a task, I would want to reduce the stigma associated with mental illnesses so that more people come forward for treatment. I would persuade people that these are health issues and take the focus away from what is happening to our minds. I would expand the scope of these health issues to encompass a higher percentage of the population and empower the medical community to prescribe certain drugs, convincing people that there is no stigma associated with taking these drugs. The *Strategy* accomplishes all this.

Before you criticize this interpretation of the *Strategy,* consider what is already happening in other countries. I read in the news and on social media outlets that certain socialistic countries are happier than we are. They pay more taxes, but their government takes care of them; they are therefore happier, or so the news attempts to convince us. Is this part of the *Strategy* or objective news coverage?

The strongest correlation to happiness in these polls, it turns out, is not the type of government but the percentage of medicated citizens. Feeling uncooperative today? Feeling discontent with the government? Why, those are signs that you might be suicidal! We can't have that. Here, take this pill. Don't want to take it? We have involuntary commitment to help you. We recommend you come with us peacefully.

What's next? Convince us it is our duty as good citizens to acquiesce, to submit, and to yield to all demands of the federal government? Is our government turning our former republic into the equivalent of a communistic or dictatorial committee while reassuring us we still have a democracy because we get to vote for the candidate of the party's choosing?

I don't want to go on a rant, just revealing how I think and how I respond to segments of the *Strategy.* I do not trust the empowerment goal.

I am not sure how many suicidals were included in the focus groups that created the *Strategy.* This *Strategy* seems to be written by professionals for professionals. If we want to create buy-in from suicidals, perhaps we should create an input process for their feedback into the next policy.

More importantly, allow empowerment to mean what it says. We need to determine our own lives, make mistakes, fail, get things wrong, and end our lives on our own terms. If empowerment doesn't mean that to you, then just tell the truth about what you intend to accomplish.

Redefine Suicide. When is a decision to end one's own life a tragedy or not a tragedy? Who gets to decide?

I know a few people who help others transition to the next life. Transition teams contribute a larger perspective from which to view life as empowered humans. They also work with families and friends in the grief process to receive the gift of the person who left. The process is triggered by someone's decision to let go, allowing their soul to leave this world for what comes next.

I don't know what comes next, but I am intrigued by the idea of people choosing to pass on. No weapons, no drugs, no rope, no knives. Select friends and family in attendance. Grief, sadness, saying good-bye—all done with intention. Is this suicide?

Suicide is often defined as the act of taking one's own life voluntarily and intentionally. If this is so, then transitioning certainly counts as suicide. However, is it a tragedy or something we should ban? I strongly believe it is neither.

Death is such a powerful, emotionally charged human experience; we tell stories of death as a grim reaper, snatching life away from people often when they least want to die. Death comes from accidents, wars, diseases, and events some people still call "acts of God," for lack, of a better explanation. We tell stories that generate fear around a natural event that none of us avoids. These are not the only stories.

In the movie *Titanic*, Jack puts Rose on the raft. When he tries to get on the raft, it flips. Realizing there is only enough buoyancy for one person, Jack makes the decision to let Rose be that person. Many people say this is their favorite scene in the movie. People cried in the movie theater, including men who don't often cry. Did Jack commit suicide? Yes, but we excuse if not romanticize a decision to die if it is for what we deem a sacrifice for someone else. Why accept suicide for this reason but not others?

Nearly two thousand years ago, a prophet (some say, more than a prophet) told his disciples, "Greater love has no one than this, that one lay down his life for his friends."[102] He also said, "I am the good shepherd; the good shepherd lays down His life for the sheep."[103] He willingly allowed himself to be killed. Was it suicide?

An injury left a man with no functioning kidneys. He needed dialysis three times per week. After many years he decided to stop the dialysis. Five days later he died. Suicide?

When people deliberately engage in a dangerous activity, we might be tempted to yell, "Don't do it! It's suicide!" If I risk my life to save someone else, people call me a hero. If I risk my life for an adrenaline rush, people label me selfish.

People who say suicide is selfish are condemning suicidals from a position of selfishness. Seems hypocritical to me. Why do your perceptions get to override mine? What moral system allows you to feel self-righteous about condemning me for thinking only of myself when, in doing so, you engage in the same process? Why does our social contract about suicide value the opinion of a friend, a doctor, or a politician about what I must do for the good of society over my autonomy to live my life or lay it down as I choose?

I want to add a discussion of selfishness and altruism to our national debate about suicide because we have these concepts backwards. By defining suicide as "tragic," we impose a dangerous moral judgment onto another individual's decision to live life on personal terms. It's a judgment that condemns that person for the very thought process we engage in to arrive at that conclusion.

While publicly touting a medical definition of suicide, many in our society privately define suicide as the ultimate in selfishness and view selfishness as immoral. Even if suicidals are selfish, that is in fact exactly the quality they need to develop healthy life choices. You want them to take care of themselves—act selfishly. Yet if they act in ways you disapprove of, you criticize and ostracize them for their selfish actions. Then you seem bewildered that they feel alone and reluctant to seek your help.

The *Strategy* wants to remove the stigma associated with suicide. Yet this same document labels suicide as "tragic." Suicides do not see their deaths as tragic but as solutions. By labeling suicide as a tragedy, we place the entire nation on one side of the discussion and suicidals on the other. We tell them that they don't see their deaths as tragic because of their mental health issues, or they are selfish, or they don't care. This dissociation, this ethical framework, this value judgment we add to the definition of suicide is part of the problem.

Under what conditions might we view suicide as a healthy choice? If you immediately reply, "Under no circumstances," so be it. That is your right. However, do not then insult my intelligence by stating you want to remove the stigma associated with suicide. I don't believe you. If asked that question in a strategic meeting, I would suggest the following for consideration:

If you choose to end your life, we ask that you:

- Use nonviolent means.
- Announce your intention in advance.
- Listen to close family, friends, and employer.
- Consider other solutions.
- Be accountable; this is your decision, so don't blame anyone else.
- Ask for what you want, knowing that no one owes you anything.
- Give us a change to say good-bye; don't die, leaving only a note.

Here is a cryptic version of a conversation with a suicidal:

"Hi, I'm Frank. How are you?"

A sign and a weak smile.

"I hear you want to end your life. I support empowering people to live their lives on their own terms, including choosing how to exit. How can I support you?"

Puzzled look. "Support me? You're not going to try to talk me out of it?"

"I would rather talk to you about your terms. What impact do you want to leave behind?"

I find that suicidals often are not actually exiting on their own terms. Perhaps they think they are, looking only at that moment of death. But when we talk about impact, message, and legacy, a bigger picture comes into view. They often want a different result but don't know how to achieve it. Living and dying with intentional expression are two sides of the same coin. Restricting one impedes the other. As we discuss how people want to die, we also expand how they might live. Dialogue about creating the elements of the crossing-over they want to experience requires that we create the life to create them. Our next step to the death they choose is the life they choose. If we can create that together, dying becomes less important.

This conversation is more cooperative, less confrontational *and*, in my opinion, more successful than telling them all the reasons they are not allowed to end their lives. This approach decreases the crisis and helps them create paths they want to follow moving forward. I start with supporting them, truly being with them in that moment, and recognizing that suicide is a legitimate choice they can make without judgments.[104]

Although their issues differ, I find that many suicidals have something in common. If they're honest with themselves, they want to be remembered for what good they've done in this world. I want that for them as well. We focus on how to accomplish it. Does this violent self-harm help people remember their amazing spark of life? Life is like a speech; the two most important parts are the conclusion and the introduction. It's too late to create a new introduction, but you can certainly create a new conclusion if this is not the one you want people to remember.

I ask suicidals how they want people to miss them and if their dying will create that result.[105] Often they see that they are not actually leaving on their own terms. They are allowing despair, the judgment of others, and stories they tell themselves about their futures to dictate the moment. I try to help them regain control of the discussion.

Conversation with a suicidal isn't about dogma, creeds, political party lines, social mores, or judgments. It's about turning their lives around. I am not willing to help people end their lives, but I will use every tool I can think of to help them regain their lives if they will work with me.

I want to reframe the national discussion to clearly state that we stand with everyone who is thinking of ending their own lives. Under what conditions will we view suicide as a healthy choice? Let us truly remove the stigma associated with suicide so that suicidals are more likely to ask for the help they need.

Increase consent requirements. When should the medical community—physical and mental— treat people against their will? The shift from viewing suicide as a health issue does not likely mean we now have the same answer for both types of conditions. What would happen if the entire medical community stopped treating people when they don't want to be treated?

I am a huge fan of the medical profession. When my daughter, Melissa, came down with spinal meningitis as a young child, I felt helpless. I would protect any of my kids from anything, but bacteria I didn't even know existed, almost took her life. I also could not afford to completely pay for the medical care from my own funds. Fortunately, our government-supported insurance program took care of the bill. I am grateful that today Melissa is a police officer and a mother of two dynamic kids. We could each share dozens of similar stories, stories of when we wanted treatment, perhaps desperately so, for either ourselves or a loved one, and our medical community did everything they could.

Medical rules and ethics require certain professionals to perform specific actions even without, and sometimes contrary to, informed consent.[106]

"Let me treat that for you."

"No thanks."

"If left untreated, it will kill you."

"I know, but no thanks."

Then what? Force treatment on me against my consent? Does it matter what *it* is? If *it* is a mental illness, the system can simply define someone as lacking mental capacity so that, by definition, they cannot consent. Then treatment may be given, regardless of my wishes, during a short internment if necessary. The state and its actors end up with all the power, and our only way out of this system seems to be the one action they want to prevent.

In the 2000 legislative session, the state of Washington passed its first mental health advance directive (MHAD) legislation. Although well intentioned, the legislation created more issues than it solved. An organization then known as the Washington Protection and Advocacy System created a team to propose revised legislation with input from patients, practitioners, care givers, facilities, other organizations advocating for people with mental illness. As part of a summer externship during my 1L summer in 2001, I worked with that team, focusing on a form we could propose in which someone with a mental illness diagnosis could consent in advance to specified treatment programs.

I started by calling organizations in the fifteen states that had already passed MHAD legislation, asked what worked, what did not, why, and what could they recommend. We then talked with stakeholders. Talking with patients opened my eyes to concerns I had not experienced or learned during my BA Psychology classes.

Their top concerns were to what extent the state could use their advanced consent to initiate confinement, medications, or treatment they didn't want. What was the most feared treatment? Electroshock therapy. The most dreaded drugs? Those that would make them not remember themselves.

Consent is a delicate balance of patient rights, family concerns, social worker duties, medical ethics and liabilities, and state interests. The consent form we designed is still part of our MHAD legislation.[107] Comparing the *Strategy* to the Washington MHAD on the topic of consent, I do not see the same level of concern or consideration of the suicidal's position at the national level.

"We're here to help you. All you have to do is consent to the treatment we prescribe."

"I don't want to be treated the way you treat people. You scare me."

"You can voluntarily consent, or we can impose involuntary treatment. Your choice."

"Not much of a choice."

And they wonder why we don't' fully embrace what they think they have to offer.

Decrease Drug Dependency. If the Veteran's administration is indicative of the National Strategy to solve mental health issues with drugs, the United States of America has a drug problem. While one department is out fighting a useless war on drugs (meaning only those drugs the government doesn't regulate for its own profit), other departments are forcing drugs on people to the extent it makes me wonder who are the truly insane. I know the word *insane* is out of vogue, but where is the voice of Susan Powers in the drug treatment debate screaming at us to stop the insanity?

My prescription drugs cause harmful side effects. What's the solution? Another drug. I know suicidals who take ten-plus prescriptions, managing thirty-plus pills per day at varying intervals. Millions of seniors in Florida might say, "You're a lightweight, you cry baby!" I get that, but it doesn't resolve the issue that our government is drugging its citizens at an alarming rate, and suicidals are at the top of the drug-dispensing hit list. What are the suicidals going to do, object? Visit the seventh floor?

Most discussions with suicidals at the Seattle VA about stopping unnecessary medications include a fear that doing so may result in a visit to the seventh floor. I have not been to the seventh floor; I don't know what happens there. Scenes from *One Flew Over the Cuckoo's Nest* come to mind. I met one woman in her twenties who told me how much she benefited from her stay. She successfully turned her life around on the seventh floor. Most suicidal veterans who share their experiences of the seventh floor do not do so with fondness or gratitude. Does this fear shape behavior? Definitely. I know that if I create another suicide attempt, I will most likely wake up in that ward.

I choose instead to live with healthy intentions, finding constructive reasons rather than fearful avoidance. Some people need to feel that fear to keep them on track, if on track includes living a life they don't fully embrace. Many of them do not want to remain in a drug treatment program. Unfortunately, our *Strategy* offers few alternatives.

How intertwined is the profit-driven drug industry with our national politics that our *Strategy* to reduce suicide includes spending billions of dollars on drugs that sometimes do more harm than good? Is suicide really so atrocious that we need to force drugs on people to turn them into someone else—a docile, placated someone, with no drive to do anything as long as that includes not committing suicide?

A study in the Baltimore area showed more than two-thirds of patients taking a prescription drug for depression never met the clinical definition of depression. Why the prescription? The study found correlations to female gender, Caucasian ethnicity, and recent or current physical problems such as loss of bladder control, hypertension, and back pain.[108]

While current medications may be safer than their predecessors, a *Harvard Health* article as recent as 2005 showed side effects for antidepressants to be as harmful as suicide.[109]

One drug helped me. Two others nearly killed me or caused me to kill myself. We have not yet looked honestly in this country at the possibility that this cure might be part of the problem. I suggest shifting our strategy from one appearing to compel our citizens to accept drugs to a government role of educating its citizens on the benefits and legitimate concerns of various approaches, and let them choose.

As a parent, I see coercion at work in other strategies such as vaccinations, where the solutions forced on our own children can prove counterproductive; yet informed parents are sometimes criticized for even raising concerns.

Vaccinations are linked to autism and SIDS and sometimes create the very diseases they are designed to counter. Yet our government seems more concerned about protecting drug companies than informing parents. In California unvaccinated children are such a danger to the rest of society that they are not allowed to attend any public education institution. I find it strange that, if vaccinations work, why do I need to fear exposure to an unvaccinated child? Reporting of adverse drug reactions (ADRs), including reactions to vaccines, are voluntary for medical providers in the US, so we do not know whether we have all of the data about potential effects.

American medical schools teach administering vaccines but not how to identify a vaccine reaction. While unofficial surveys suggest that highly vaccinated children may have more chronic health problems than unvaccinated children, unvaccinated children have a far lower incidence rate of autism, and vaccines may be associated with a variety of brain and immune system disorders, our CDC has never (won't?) created an official study to compare health outcomes of vaccinated versus unvaccinated children. Meanwhile, a study from China says that 42 percent of the ADRs reported by their medical community were from vaccinations.[110]

I am not trying to resolve the vaccine debate here, although I also think that strategy could use a shift toward more patient rights. I mention it here to demonstrate another way our national policies favor drugs over both patients' rights and non-drug alternatives. I strongly believe our *National Suicide Strategy's* incorporation of a pro-drug policy is part of the suicide problem.

Fortunately, non-drug treatments are increasing. The cognitive behavioral therapy and intensive outpatient program I participated in at the VA are stellar examples. A recent breakthrough government-funded study, the most rigorous trial to date conducted in the United States, concluded that schizophrenia patients who participated in a program intended to keep dosages of antipsychotic medication as low as possible, emphasizing one-on-one talk therapy and family support, made greater strides in recovery over the first two years of treatment than patients who got the usual drug-focused care.[111]

It makes so much sense that one wonders why we need a study, but our insistence on "scientific" solutions is an issue for another time. The good news is we are moving in the right direction, away from drugs and toward a more holistic approach. I hope future strategy discussions in general will place a greater emphasis on such solutions.

A Culture of Caring. We reject death at all costs. The idea that we will die one day, but today is not that day resonates as a battle cry in numerous epic movies. We behave as if life itself contains a duty to resist death, never succumbing and forcing death to take us. We die in the ultimate battle of life as heroes. When we pass, it is said of us that we lost a battle with cancer,[112] or we met with a tragic accident. The one death that does not elevate drama is the death of someone of advanced years, at home, in the arms of loved ones.

Our centuries-old dance with death and dying created dance steps we all follow, like footprints on the floor at an Arthur Murray studio. We demand that medical professionals prevent dying to the best of their abilities, and we oblige our citizens to do everything possible to remain alive. I recommend changing both.

Which is more compassionate: treating someone with prescriptions or procedures that kill the quality of live while maintaining a physical presence or supporting someone to live the remainder of life in a positive, happy way?

Henry Marsh, author and one of Britain's preeminent neurosurgeons, asks to what extent we should treat people with advanced cancers in the hope of prolonging life. "Most of us would accept a great deal of suffering in hope of a cure. The issue is whether doctors should subject patients to unpleasant non-curative treatments. To my mind there is no question that we are overtreating at the moment."[113]

I do not blame the medical profession for overtreating. We created this result. Doctors want to talk to their patients about healthy life choices, but we don't want to hear it. We don't want to change our habits or our life styles. We want to continue behaviors our medical profession tells us will create unhealthy results, but then we demand from them a pill or procedure that will wipe away the consequences.

I can only imagine what we, as patients, might say if a doctor recommended preparing for death. We demand that they continue down any path toward not dying, no matter how small the chances. "Not dying" is more important in our culture than living, and most of us do not even see the two as different.

We take an umbrella in case it rains, we pack extra food and water on trips, and we buy stocks for capital gains yet cover them with options in case the price falls. In every area of our lives we plan for contingencies. But if a doctor says there is only a small chance of success, we refuse to even consider our death. Plan for death? Not in our culture.

Atul Gawande, American surgeon, author, and public health researcher, writes about our fixation for a solution to avoid death, even when we have a terminal illness.

> What's wrong with looking for it? Nothing, it seems to me, unless it means we have failed to prepare for the outcome that's vastly more probable. The trouble is that we've built our medical system and culture around the long tail [of possibility]. We've created a multi-trillion dollar edifice for dispensing the medical equivalent of lottery tickets – and have only the rudiments of a system to prepare patients for the near certainty that those tickets will not win. Hope is not a plan, but hope is our plan.[114]

We need a better plan. The perfection demanded of our medical system and inherent in the *Strategy's* zero suicides goal, is part of the problem. The medical profession, those we consult to prevent suicide, has the highest rate of suicide of any professional group. Danielle Ofri, physician and writer, refers to the "tyranny of perfection" as a primary cause.[115]

Rather than decrease the vulture culture in medicine, whoever develops strategies for the medical profession initiated a Physician's Help Program (PHP) to help them deal with stress. Physicians complain that members of their professional community who voluntarily disclose they have mental health problems can be forced into treatment without recourse; they can face expensive out-of-pocket costs and can be required to receive the prescribed therapy out of state. The PHP system itself makes doctors more reluctant to admit mental health issues.[116]

I find this is also true in the veteran community: the commendable *Strategy* goal of reducing the stigma associated with self-reporting is defeated by the system itself.

A study from the United Kingdom linked British regulatory process to both suicidal thoughts in physicians and defensive practice procedures such as overprescribing.[117] I imagine the same is true for our system, although our tort liability system might add more anxiety here than in the UK.

Our next *Strategy* should look at ways to reduce tensions in our provider and reporting systems. I strongly believe we should also learn to deal with death as the 100 percent probable conclusion it is to living. What if we create a healthy way to discuss dying? We could engage suicidals in a conversation about what a salubrious ending looks like. The motivation is not to assist them in their suicide but help them walk through a process of creating the end they truly want. Most people want their deaths to end peacefully, not in a medicated or violent condition.

What can we do to help them create that? Perhaps cross suicide prevention with doula end-of-life training.[118] Let us at least allow, if not promote, healthy discussions about death, dying, and what death by suicide looks like versus other choices one could make. Helping create the life they want is the same conversation as supporting them to create the death experience they truly desire.

A shift away from imposing on our citizens a duty to remain alive, no matter what the consequences to their quality of life, is simply reflecting the reality that they owe no such duty to others in positions of authority. When interacting with suicidals, one of the most powerful gifts we can give them is to help them create their own reasons to live. "You must stay alive for the benefit of others" is not a strong reason and will often turn them away. By eliminating mandates on suicidals for our communal benefit we then need to rethink our own reasons why we engage suicidals at all.

If someone represented a state or national perspective when interacting with a suicidal, what do we want that person to say?

"We don't want you to end your life."

"Why do you care?"

~~"Think of the economic loss."~~

~~"Your nation / family / community need you."~~

~~"Our stats look bad when stacked against other nations."~~

~~"It's my job to stop you so I won't let you kill yourself."~~

"I care because ..."

When we have a national answer to the last question, let's add it to the *Strategy*. The other answers don't work. I don't see a message of caring in the current *Strategy*, and I don't always hear it implemented at the street level.

When we shift away from viewing suicide prevention as an obligation of suicidals to supporting them in creating the life they want because we care, we will indeed see a dramatic drop in suicide rates. Suicide notes frequently contain the theme of an uncaring world. Let's create a caring ethos so strong that everyone in our country, no matter how isolated, can hear the message.

I don't mean advertising a "We Care" tagline merely to increase public perception. How do we back it up, demonstrate it, walk the talk, show what we mean, and reinforce our intention with resources and action plans? Make it a central theme of our next *Strategy*. It might prove to be the only theme we need.

Suicide on a National Spectrum. Let's return to the spectrum one more time.

–10 (Suicide)   (Life) +10

Our national number on this scale, while difficult to calculate, is as, if not more, important as the total number of suicides. Just as an individual and a community can move in a positive direction, so can our nation. The number of suicides then becomes one test measure of how well we are living as a national community, rather than a primary focus.

What does it take to move a country as large and diverse as the

USA toward more life? Sebastian Junger believes the answer lies in addressing our bitterly divided modern society. I fully agree with Junger when he states, "Maybe what determines the rate of long-term PTSD isn't what happened out there, but the kind of society you come back to. And maybe if you come back to a close, cohesive, tribal society, you can get over trauma pretty quickly. And if you come back to an alienating, modern society, you might remain traumatized your entire life. In other words, maybe the problem isn't them, the vets; maybe the problem is us."[119]

Yes, the suicide problem rests in us, as a national community. It is inherent in our negatively divisive culture, constantly isolating people into smaller and smaller groups until many people feel alone in a country of over 300 million people. Realizing this, we can also be the solution.

Our country needs a healthier national identity, one in which we support each other during disagreements because what unites us is stronger than what divides us. Let's build a country where every American can be proud of his or her country. Let's fashion an efficacious ethos that enables other multicultural countries to look to us a model for successfully uniting a free people.

I recommend we start in Washington, DC. Let us demand and support leaders who coalesce in decision making and empower others. Let us reject politicians looking to cement their own political power by keeping the country turned against itself. We will have disagreements on how best to mold our future and work together, as we did during the American Revolution and during the world wars. Our common enemy now is not a military powerhouse, asserting its mandates on unwilling populations; it is internal strife that undermines cultural cohesiveness and replaces it with hopeless malaise.

Statistics for 2015 show that suicide rates increased in 2014. According to one behavioral science professor, the increase indicates a "persistent lack of robust treatment infrastructure in this country."[120] Yes, it can indicate that, and I find it fully appropriate for a behavioral science professor to think along those lines. As a patient of the treatment infrastructure in this country, though, I am amazed at the resources available if suicidals will commit to living. I find this statistic more indicative of a disenfranchised populace, a national shift toward –10.

Now is the time to turn this around. Now is the time to create an inclusive, welcoming vision of American society. Some of my friends tell me it is too late and that we have passed a point of no return. I do not believe it. If I can turn my life around, and if others can reverse the trajectory of their communities, we can do the same for our country. We will need to work together, as if our lives and the future of our country depend on it.

Individuals Influencing the National Culture

In one sense the *Strategy* is not relevant. The government did not create this problem, and we don't need their leadership to solve the issue. If suicides didn't happen, we wouldn't need our government to create a *Strategy*. We, as suicidals and those who care about them, can create a national community, bolstered by millions of smaller communities, where people become invested in their own lives to the extent that suicide holds no interest. Will this prevent all suicides? I don't know, but I do know it will make a difference, and that's a good place to start.

To balance a chemical formula, one can often simply add some of the opposite. Is it heavily alkaline? Add an acid. Are we surrounded by darkness? Add light. Are we mired in a culture of death? Add life.

This is your new mission, your new *raison d'être*: inject life into the world every day. Influence others to join you. There are hundreds of ways you can add life to our world. Three of my favorites follow. If any of them resonate with you or if you feel some energy building as you read them, you've found a purpose worth living for. We need you!

Zoé Life

You're walking on a city street. Flowers sold by a street vendor open in glorious bloom as you walk by. Birds start singing as you stroll under a tree. People say hello and smile. Squirrels stop chattering and wave. One shares an acorn by dropping it in front of you. You notice a couple walking toward you, grim expressions being the only revelation of their sadness. As you pass them, he turns to her, smiles weakly, and tells her, "I do love you, more than I admit. I don't want that situation to come between us!" and they embrace. If asked later what influenced him to heal the disconnect he felt with her, he won't know; it was just a feeling. This is the life you bring everywhere you go![121]

I sometimes find the English language confusing and restrictive. We have words that apply to only one item, such as the smell of rain after a dry spell (*petrichor*) and the plastic tip at the end of a shoelace (*aglet*). Yet we use words such as *life* and *love* in so many situations that we make the words almost meaningless.

In *Koine* Greek classes, I learned three words for life: βίος (bios), ψυχή (psuche), and ζωὴ (zoe). Koine is an older Greek language active at the time of the New Testament. Greeks of that era used *bios* to describe the physical aspects of life (think biology and biography), *psuché* for the breath of life, the human soul, the self of an individual (psychology); and *zoé,* the essence, quality, or concept of life itself.

The Greeks described people as balancing different life energies. What exactly is *zoé* life or energy? Imagine a container of energy that keeps us moving during the day. It's not the physical energy of muscles feeling tired after hard labor or the mental energy of knowing we can do something. It is that energy born of purpose, desire, and the reason why. I don't know whether *zoé* is stored in our bodies or if it's just a construct, but I often view it as residing in a pool—an artesian well—a resource we can call on any time.

What does life look like if that resource runs dry? How can we prime the pump to restart the life flow? It is not a secret; we already know the answer. *Zoé* works like yeast, like giving someone a starter of friendship bread, like a mountain spring so full it overflows to become a resource of life, yielding grass in an alpine meadow for deer to eat and continuing its flow for farmers to water crops.

We know people like this, people so full of life that the essence of life in nature and people and situations around them respond with recognition. Imagine a community full of such people—vibrant, alive, energetic, creative, and harmonious. Easy for them, you say. Perhaps that's just their nature. What if life-adding energy is everyone's essential nature? Imagine how different our world would be if seven billion people decided every day to inject life into their surroundings. This one concept, by itself, could end suicide on a global scale.

I met a woman in a city project area who was tending a flower bed on her small patio. I complimented her on her flowers. She beamed, expressed her thanks, and said this was her way of adding color in her neighborhood. We can add hugs, smiles, and a helping hand to any situation that needs one and to people we know or strangers who cross our paths.

This is the *real* life movement: doctors or dentists going into other countries that lack essential services,[122] high school students traveling around the world to bring energetic hope and encouragement to everyone they meet,[123] and people working together to help someone on the street have a hot meal and a bed for a night.[124] You, smiling at a stranger you pass on the street, may add enough life to their container to help them put off suicide for one more day.

Some people are surprised to discover that, with my views on life, I do not support the pro-life movement. I would rather live in a world where abortions are legal and don't happen than one in which they are illegal and happen anyway. Our society does not need to prosecute medical providers or mothers for terminating a pregnancy. I appreciate that movement's focus on when human life begins. It depends on how we define *life*—life as human *bios*? Or does it begin at conception, the same way a particular molecular structure's existence creates headlines about life on Mars? When do the *psuché* or *zoé* aspects of human life begin?

A baby fully depends on its mother for all aspects of its life. What does an anti-abortion law accomplish in terms of the baby's existence? We know that nutrition plays a key role in prenatal development. After denying access to an abortion, do we then force the mother to eat nutritious meals, drink plenty of water, rest appropriately, read to her growing offspring, speak to it, love it unconditionally, or any of the other myriad activities a loving mother does instinctively?

What do we gain with the political pro-life movement? You who give money to pro-life causes, do you care about the life that baby will live after it's born? Do you care about the effects of poverty, malnutrition, lack of access to health care, or other essential services? You applaud yourselves with every regulatory restriction on abortions, but, from what I can tell, you exhibit little concern for human life as an overall concept. You don't deserve the name *pro-life;* it's a misnomer compared to what you accomplish. You should call yourselves the anti-abortion movement because that's all you do. Leave the pro-life moniker for those of us who value life in all its glory and strive to add life to every moment we can.

If any pro-choice people are applauding that paragraph, don't pat yourselves on the back just yet. Your definition of human life is even worse. You are so focused on ensuring a woman doesn't feel guilty about having an abortion that you treat a developing human being with all the dignity of a kidney stone. I applaud the health care and prenatal services provided by organizations such as Planned Parenthood, but I detest the abortion industry. Have you seen a picture of a baby at twelve weeks?[125] How can you then honestly discuss abortion in terms of anything other than terminating a human life? That baby is not a cancer, an infectious gland, or a benign tumor. It's a person, endowed with all the components of human life and fully dependent on not just its mother but everyone in its small community to get it to the next level.

Does a mother have a choice to end that human life? Yes, just as people have a choice to end their own lives. I don't want laws criminalizing abortion any more than I want one criminalizing suicide. Not passing laws to criminalize either is a divisive enough issue, but it's easy by comparison to drawing the line on taxpayer support for services such as abortions or medically assisted suicide. Are these services only for those who can afford them or will we, as a society, make them available to people who cannot? If we do, under what circumstances?

For me, the abortion rules in our country are too broad, and the assisted suicide laws are too restrictive. This writing is not the place to decide these issues. Please take a deep breath and relax a moment. I bring it up not to alienate a huge segment of the readers but to stimulate thinking about how we define life. Breathe, pause, and come back to our discussion of adding life when you're ready.

...

Welcome back. Is it enough to say that we prevented a suicide today if the person who chose not to end his or her life is merely sent back to the same circumstances that will recreate the same desire to end life tomorrow?

In some sense an unborn child is a microcosm analogous to a suicidal's environment. We do not cease to be dependent on others the day we are born. All the nutrition, love, kindness, warmth, and safety needed by a baby apply to all of us throughout our lives. Our lives intersect, connect, and flow in more ways than we realize. We are all part of the suicide problem, and we are all part of the solution.

One does not need to live a monastic life to be part of the *zoé* real-life movement. Every day we live is a day to suit up and play the game of life. How will you show up today?

Perhaps your *zoé* well is dry. You can't bring life to others from an empty spring. Some of my Baptist friends will say this is the time for an altar call. No, I have seen too many paths for renewing one's life force to limit my recommendation to that one method. We live those values by stepping off our street corner boxes, leaving our altars God never asked us to hide behind, and getting out into the world to bring love and kindness to strangers. Priming the pump of your *zoé* tank is simple. Turn on the switch by taking action. The power already exists. You are designed to circulate life. Life is part of your nature.

If you need a starter—that first bit of water to get the pump flowing, that small ball of friendship bread that will soon have you wondering what to do with all your bread—seek and ye shall find. When I need a boost, I listen to inspiring music, walk, play with my dog, or listen to my grandkids laugh. I also find it by reading or meditating (the same thing as prayer, in my opinion). We also get it from other people. For help getting started, ask someone you admire to share this quality with you.

Then, when you're ready, decide how you want to show up in the world. Get down with your bad self. Wear purple, dance, put on outrageous socks, say hi to a stranger, and get out of your comfort zone. Live! Be the person you want to be, live your mission, and help others do the same. We're all in this world together, and we need each other if we want to go beyond mere survival to abundant life for all.

Economic Life

Talking someone through a suicidal episode and then sending them back into the same environment in which they feel powerless, angry, and depressed often seems to me like Linus and Charlie Brown noticing a freezing Snoopy and encouraging him with a hearty "Be of good cheer, Snoopy!" Unless we can help people change their environments and the ways they think about them, we will see them again, struggling with the same suicidal thoughts.

A few minutes ago, I heard a TV announcer begin her segment with the statement, "Our thoughts are with the people of France [recent terrorist attack in Paris], and we offer them peace." We *offer?* I turned off the TV. It might be just me, but I judged (harshly perhaps) her statement as disingenuous. What if France takes her up on her offer? What is she going to do? My guess is she can't back up her offer because it's empty and hollow, merely a hope or wish for something she has not even bothered considering how to create. She is not capable of giving peace to France. I see her statement as insincere posturing.

Too often today sentiment gets credit for being action, as if wanting a result or feeling a particular way are enough. A presidential candidate says he wants to help the poor and blames the rich for the demise of the lower class, and people vote based on that sentiment, without having any action plan that actually helps. Sure, the powers that be formulate policies, tax people, create more high-paying federal jobs, and find one or two people who have been helped to parade before the national cameras. Yet they find it necessary to redefine unemployment so that the numbers don't look as bad after passing an unemployment stimulus package that didn't work. They change how they tally people not covered by health care to justify their takeover of the healthcare industry, even though overall numbers have not changed. They also stop counting certain groups of veterans in suicide studies to help demonstrate that DOD efforts to stem military-related suicides are working. Is it any wonder so many Americans today don't trust their own government? Many suicidals I know see national statements about suicide as the same insincere posturing displayed by the reporter.

How would we change our national priorities if we were sincere about ending suicide in our country?

We've seen pictures of bankers and stock brokers jumping from Wall Street buildings during the Great Depression. Although we don't necessarily see people jumping from buildings, suicide, as a result of economic crisis, continues. When we look at suicide across economic spectrums in the US, the two most affected groups are the poorest and the wealthiest.[126]

Research on homelessness in the UK showed that the homeless population is nine times more likely to commit suicide than the general population.[127]

I know wealthy people who do not see the poor killing themselves as a tragedy, and I know poor people who blame the rich for their plight and seem happy when an upper class person commits suicide (except people who make us laugh, like Robin Williams). Some of our national politicians, including our current president and many of our presidential candidates, actively promote this kind of class warfare to further their own political careers. The value of people's lives and the catastrophe of their suicides should not depend on their economic strata.

One of the ways we need to change our national priorities is to start by changing the dialogue. All lives, from all economic levels, are equally important. The wealthy are not to blame for the plight of the poor any more than the poor are to blame for any miseries associated with a rich lifestyle.

This is a tough issue for me because I strongly believe our federal government is too large and consumes too much of the US economy. Between federal income tax and payroll taxes, 45 percent of the money I make in my small, solo legal practice goes to the US government. And yet the government is running a debt that is currently 108 percent of the entire gross domestic product. Instead of dealing with the debt in the same responsible fashion they demand of us (ever tried paying your income tax with an IUO?), Congress just increases its own debt limit, pushing the problem further into the future.[128] This is economic suicide. I do not want to propose just adding another government program. We need a government revision if we want to truly solve the economic suicide issues because our current economic policies are part of the problem.

There are numerous successful models we can analyze for assistance in this quest. One I am most familiar with is the King County levy to end homelessness. Although not directly aimed at suicide, one of the tangential goals of the intention to end homeless in King County was to decrease its suicide numbers. When added to a list of the ten largest counties in the US, King County ranked third highest in suicide rates.[129] I am not aware of a study that looked at decreases in the suicide rates as a result of the efforts to end homelessness.

King County voters passed the homeless ballot measure in November 2005. Half the revenue raised funds services for veterans, military personnel, and their families, including services specific to veterans' needs such as treatment for post-traumatic stress disorder. The other half funded regional health and human services, including housing, homelessness prevention, mental health and substance abuse services, and employment assistance.

A Veterans and Human Services Implementation ordinance received approval by the King County Council on April 10, 2006. The legislation required a service improvement plan outlining the use of the levy proceeds, clarified the roles and process for appointing the members of the citizen's oversight boards, and required the county to reexamine priorities, policies, and contracts for human services currently funded with county discretionary funds. I was an initial member of the board created with oversight for the veteran's funds.

The levy identified three goal areas for service enhancement and funding allocations: reduce homelessness and emergency medical costs, reduce criminal justice system involvement, and increase self-sufficiency by means of employment. The creators of the levy idea believed that addressing these goals would result in both a decrease in homelessness and overall savings to the King County budget, with offsetting decreases in the criminal justice and social services budgets. King County also created a Veteran's Court to steer veterans into social services programs (such as the federally funded VA, a different way of decreasing the county budget) rather than prison for issues linked to PTSD.

Like any government program, the first levy dollars funded two new King County administrative positions. I did not like that reality, but programs need staff to properly administer them.

Utah also implemented a program to end homelessness around that same time. I joked at a levy board meeting once that the easiest and least expensive way for us to end homelessness in Seattle was to buy all our homeless a bus pass to Salt Lake City. Mathematically it would end homelessness in our area for a short time, but a real solution isn't that simple. Solving homelessness is also not as simple as stating that Salt Lake City ended their homelessness by purchasing hundreds of small sheds that look like miniature homes.[130] What about electricity, running water, bathrooms, or simply a mailing address? I know people who believe buying sheds is all we need to do to end homelessness. By a strict definition of the word, yes, but he only difference between a shed they occupy and a cardboard box under a bridge they call "theirs" is that we have something pretty to look at, so we don't see them. Then we feel better about ourselves and tell ourselves our job is done.

Solving chronic suicide is even more complicated. We can walk around a city and identify homeless people. We can't circulate through a crowd and spot suicidals. Some of the services that chronic suicidals need overlap with chronic homelessness, but suicide is less economic in nature. I took a suicidal vet to lunch a few days ago. She tells people that, with over thirty suicide attempts in her life, she is perhaps the worst suicidal ever. The purpose of lunch was not to interview her for the book but to collaborate on a local workshop to help raise awareness on some issues. But, during our conversation, I felt inspired by her story. Six months since her most recent (and she believes last) suicide attempt, she is happy and in a stable living situation. She has a small income and a monthly disability check from the VA, a car she can't afford to fix, access to public transportation, and friends who give her rides to church. Might circumstances devolve to look similar to circumstances where, in the past, she decided to end her life? Perhaps, but now she has a plan, resources to implement that plan, and people who care about her who will check up on her. Most importantly, she exudes a strong reason to live; she has a life energy that attracts people, where it used to repel them and isolate her. I see her as one of the most successful suicidals ever.

Adding economic life is not just about dollars or services, although these are important. It's about economic vitality and self-sustainability; it's about people feeling like they are in control of their lives rather than being dependent. It's about the systems we want to create in our society that allow people access to help they need when they need it. The economic hopelessness that leads to suicide depends less on one's personal net worth than on one's perceived ability to do something about one's economic condition—whatever the circumstances.

Over the past several years (some might argue decades), our national government moved our economy further away from the independence we, as Americans, are born into, toward government control, entitlement, and redistribution. We continue to increase our national debt and spending to the point where the burden of supporting our government starts looking more like the futility felt by a feudal serf. Our representative government treats us as if the only thing we are capable of doing is electing them into office; it divides us into groups and sets us against each other rather than leading us into working together toward common prosperity. I don't want to come across here as Nathan confronting David or John the Baptist challenging Herod, but when I look at the economic issues created by our federal government and their impact on people, I see DC as the source of many reasons for our suicide numbers. Yet when I read the *Strategy*, I do not see those factors acknowledged or addressed.

One month ago a company I did contract legal work for decided it did not want a vet with PTSD/suicidal issues as part of its legal team. It's ironic that they discovered my issues because I told them as part of my recovery. At the time they let me go, I was a better, stronger part of their team than ever before, but that's not how they viewed it. Another vet with similar issues lost his security job in a school district. I get it. Suicidals are a tough group to employ. Some of us are comedians, a few of them remarkably successful. Society loves them. The rest of us—not so much.

After losing my income last month, I decided to start a financial services business. Potential agents need to be able to pass a background check, pay for licensing and Errors & Omissions coverage, and present complex financial issues in a straightforward manner. So we are not going to accept just any suicidal, but a PTSD diagnosis and past suicide attempts are not a barrier to working with my company. I feel more empowered and excited about my own financial future now, even though I don't know how we are going to pay the bills this month. I don't feel suicidal at all; I feel energized! It's a huge change from the past when not having enough money to pay bills resulted in suicidal actions.

Solving the economic aspect of suicide is about empowerment, freedom, and opportunity. It's not just about equal opportunity but ample opportunity, showing people how they can release themselves from the yokes placed on their shoulders.

When working with suicidals, I love to ask them about what they want to do.

> Me: If you could do anything you want, what do you want to do?

Answer: I want to be part of the leisure class, where I can shop, sail, travel, and do whatever I want and have all the money I need to do it.

Me: Is that where you are at?

A: No! (laughter)

Me: Do you see a way to get there?

A: No. (sadness)

Me: How do you know you'll be happy when you get there? I know people who live that lifestyle and are not happy.

A: (silence)

I heard this scenario numerous times. That lifestyle is often not what people truly want and it will not necessarily make them happy. Money helps, but is not the issue. Let's think about empowerment and control.

Me: Are you in control of your life?

Answer: I'm not in control. I don't like what I do. I'm living paycheck to paycheck and can't afford to change anything.

Me: Let's ignore the "but can't afford" for a moment and just look at not liking what you do. What would you like to do?

A: Sell exotic cars! (Excitement in their eyes and voice)

Me: Do you know anyone who sells exotic cars?

A: Yes! My friend Omar sells Ferraris and—

If you're on the right track, you can't keep them quiet. It's a very different result. When we identify people's passions, we can look at skill sets, training, internships, and any resources that may be available during a transition. I am amazed at how many times people are happier with scenarios where they might end up with less money, although often following their passion leads to greater economic success.

Economic life is a combination of more empowerment, less entitlement; more opportunity, less confinement; allowing people to keep more of the results of their creative energy rather than surrendering most of it as tribute. We are all in this together, and we can work together to create our own solutions. The government will catch up to us later.

Political Life

In some sense the book started with this section—my moral injury about the reality that the Iraq war was not about bringing freedom and democracy to the people of Iraq. Our government sold the war on two fronts: Saddam's potential support of terrorism, using Iraq's WMD technology (they did have some old WMD materials although not the mushroom cloud scenario depicted in our pre-war public relations) and bringing freedom to people oppressed by a crazy dictator. I volunteered to go to Iraq because I value political freedom and believed the narrative about our sacrifices to bring political freedom to people unable to create it for themselves.

Taking American revolutionary history as my reference, I thought that toppling the Saddam government would result in Iraqis holding discussions, electing delegates, forming their own constitution, and setting up interim governments as they decided necessary. That is not what happened. We set up their American-looking government for them and found Iraqis to fill the positions we fashioned. Iraqis I spoke with absolutely wanted Saddam gone. They expressed gratitude that we ousted Saddam on their behalf. At the same time, they were angry about the government we handed them. We decided what their government would look like, who we wanted to work with, and created their government for them. Iraqis did not appreciate our installation of a US-style government and giving them no option but to cooperate.

Our government circulated pictures of Iraqis smiling and raising purple fingertips to indicate they voted. We called that a success, evidence that democracy worked in Iraq. Yet in the Anbar province, during my second tour, the provincial government collected its per diem checks without passing a budget since being installed. The federal government did not fund services in that province, and the courts were closed due to Al-Qaeda Iraq (AQI) targeting judges who presided over any cases involving AQI members. And we worked to ensure that Iraqis backed the same people we supported. At every level the government we created for them did not work. Fortunately, the Iraqi people continued to demonstrate the resilience that allowed them to endure as one of the world's longest-standing cultures. They relied on their tribal system to conduct business, but their heralded voting accomplished little.

Saddam Hussein was a democratically elected president of Iraq. In 2002 he won reelection with 100 percent voter turnout in favor of electing him to another seven-year term. We discounted that as a democratic, free election with good reason; there was only one candidate, and that candidate routinely murdered opponents. The penalty for slandering that sole candidate was to have one's tongue cut out. Still, there was an election, and Iraqis voted. In fact, the Ba'ath party, under which Saddam rose to power, gave Iraqis the right to vote, not the U.S.

The post-World War I division of the Ottoman Empire created new countries in the Middle East including Iraq. A Hashemite monarchy was organized under British protection in 1921, and on October 3, 1932, the kingdom of Iraq was granted independence. Not surprisingly, the Iraqi government maintained close economic and military ties with Britain. In 1958 the monarchy was overthrown. The new Iraqi Republic was headed by a revolutionary council, with a three-man sovereignty council. It was composed of members of Iraq's three main communal/ethnic groups and acting as its president. The cabinet represented a broad spectrum of Iraqi political movements. How the 1958 Iraqi government, created by the Iraqis themselves, devolved into the 2002 one-choice-for-all election contains some important lessons for reforming American democracy.

Our government created American allegiance puppets in Iraq, and Iraqis knew it. When I looked at the Iraq government through their eyes, I noticed similarities to our political process. I also learned it was not the first elected government we've overthrown to protect American interests.[131]

In 2008 Representative Ron Paul announced he would run for president on the Republican ticket. At the time I supported the Republican Party and volunteered at the King County level. One of my brothers actively supported Ron Paul in a different county where Ron Paul supporters galvanized the precinct committee officer positions to win support at their county convention. I witnessed the State GOP craft the 2008 convention in a way that specifically disenfranchised Ron Paul supporters. The state leaders, perhaps wanting recognition by national leaders for doing a good job to enhance their own political power, did not want to waste their time with a grass roots movement—the real voice of the people. George W. Bush received the nomination, as was intended from the beginning by the top of the GOP political pyramid. Democrats witnessed the same power in action during the 2016 national primary.

If I was a member of a small group of people that wanted to control a country without fear of detection or revolution, I would create a system that looks like the American one. Allow people choices but only of preselected candidates. Not a one-party system but two, each with distinct characteristics that would draw most of the population to one camp or the other. Then, I would keep people focused on what divides them in a way that they wouldn't notice the long-term trend that, no matter who they select, the bidding of the invisible elite would always be carried out. I would convince people that the true measure of democracy is the ability to vote and that whatever their elected officials decide is, by definition, the will of the people. Then we wouldn't need to measure democracy by how accurately it represents the people's views. They voted, so the representatives they chose (carefully preselected) represent the will of the people. Except that they don't.

What if the people pulling political strings behind the scenes in each party are the same people? They allow other political parties and candidates because it helps bolster the mirage that we have a true democracy. Anyone achieving a certain measure of success that threatens the establishment will be crushed. They don't murder the opposition (officially) or cut off tongues. However, they will not hesitate to spend millions to destroy the reputation, credit, and credibility of anyone who challenges them. I now believe that a true government of the people, for the people, and by the people ended decades ago. Yes, we vote, but our voting no more accomplishes the will of the people than the votes cast by Iraqis under their new "freedom."

How can we bring life back to American democracy? Is there a way to restore a government that is truly of, for, and by the people? Yes. Veterans and non-veterans alike, morally outraged about our nation's intrusions in other countries at the expense of their democracy, are the best people to accomplish this task.

Political posture. How we fight America's next revolution is as important as the fight itself. Let's learn some lessons from the Civil War. The people who don't agree with us are part of the debate. They are Americans, and their voice is allowed in our democratic arena. We will not silence them. We will ensure that our voice and all voices are heard. This is not a battle fought with guns. We might be labeled "anti-American" or against our form of government and will therefore be ostracized or designated a threat to national security. We might be arrested for nothing more than speaking out against those who stole our power. But we are not afraid. We almost died by our own hands, so their threats mean nothing to us. We will stand firm in our integrity.

We will not use violence, period. We will not blow up buildings; we paid for them and need them in our new democracy. We merely want to shift the political power back to the voter, the American citizen, the taxpayer.

Treat all voters the same. I grew up in Canada and did not understand the history and differences between the two US political parties. After moving to the US, I stopped by our local congressman's office to ask how to become involved as a new citizen. He asked my party affiliation. When I told him I did not know, he asked me a few questions about what I believed, and, based on my answers, said that I sounded like a Republican. He then explained that the congressman was a Democrat and told me how to find the local Republican office.

Years later, as a single dad, I contemplated signing up for welfare. Predisposed by my protestant work ethic upbringing, I did not want a government hand-out. But as a single dad with three small children, relying on the wages of a dairy farm hand, I could not stretch our funds to pay for rent, utilities, and food. Standing in line outside the welfare office, someone approached with a clip board and asked me if I was registered to vote. I said no. She asked me what party I supported. I replied "Republican." She then blasted me, "Why are you in this line? Republicans are against welfare!" She would not register me and tried to shame me out of the line.

We might say that both parties do this, so in the end everyone gets registered, but why is party affiliation part of our voter registration process? Every person eligible to vote should have an opportunity to register, and people who move or pass away need to be removed from the rolls. Our election auditors should be impartial and non-partisan people who bring their impeccable integrity into the process and ensure an accurate as possible voter registration. Every eligible voter deserves a voice in a proper democracy.

Count votes correctly. In 2004 I lived in King County, Washington and actively supported a gubernatorial candidate. I fully expected Dino

Rossi to win that election, and the initial count projected he would indeed be the next governor by a few hundred votes. King County, which, based on its population, controls much of Washington politics, found ten thousand ballots that were not part of the initial submission. Court cases reminiscent of the Florida ballot in 2000 began. The US Department of Justice looked into fraud allegations, but no charges were filed.

At that time, King County was the only Washington state county where the auditor was not independently elected. Christine Gregoire became our governor in a clean election. I had no problem with that and supported her as the duly elected governor. I think if there was any tampering, Governor Gregoire was not involved, and would not sanction any. I also suspect that the Democratic Party machine in King County wanted to ensure their candidate's election, and they did their job well. Enough ballots appeared in all sorts of ways.[132] Following that election, the citizens of King County created an initiative to change the Auditor's position to one that is independently elected rather than appointed. They also changed the ballot process to mail only.

Tamper proof? It's hard to say. Is it a move in the right direction and more responsive to the citizens? Definitely. A successful democracy needs every county in every state to run clean elections and educate voters on how to successfully participate under local rules.

Defund the major political parties. Scenario: A local woman gets elected by knocking on doors and attending local fundraisers; everyone knows her and thinks highly of her, and the district sends her to DC with a grand send-off. Shortly after arrival, she meets the party chair (does not matter which party) who congratulates her on getting elected and then tells her how she is going to get reelected. The games begin. Does the party ask her to look after her district, to represent her constituents honorably, and pledge their support to help her do her job? You might be surprised, but no. That is not the nature of the conversation. She is informed that if she wants to get on the best committees, if she wants party funds, if she does not want party opposition next time, then she needs to follow the party line and vote as she is told. Our national parties want the individuals we elect to represent us to instead represent the party. Why do we put up with this?

In 2008 Kay Hagan (D) defeated Elizabeth Dole (R) to represent North Carolina in the Senate. Incumbents are considered most vulnerable in their first reelection or after a distasteful scandal. In 2014 North Carolina House Speaker Thom Tillis ran against her. The national Democratic Party spent over $11 million against Tillis, the Republicans nearly $9 million against Hagan, each party's highest 'against' expenditure for that cycle. By contrast, the GOP spent less than $500,000 for Tillis and the Democrats around $850,000 for Hagan. This pattern happens every election cycle; this election is merely an example.

Please notice two things. The first is how much more money is spent on negative advertising than positive. Why? Because it works. The parties are not going to stop negative ads until we refuse to vote as a response to negative ads.

If you are going to financially support a party, then tell that party next year you won't do so if it participates in any negative campaigning. Then if it does, cancel your support. When enough people do this, we'll change the parties and the rules.

The second is the origin of those funds. Do you believe that all the money spent by each party to influence the North Carolina election was raised in North Carolina? Not even close. If a candidate ran on a platform of returning political power to the people and everyone in that person's district contributed the maximum allowed by law, national parties and PACs could outspend that candidate in opposition advertising. Let's get in their way by working to limit their funds and the way they can spend their money.

We could prohibit taxpayer funds from covering party expenditures. In the news at the time of this writing is an AP article that Florida Congresswoman and Democratic National Committee Chairwoman Debbie Wasserman Schultz drafted a bill to restore money that both parties received in the past from the federal government to help defray the costs of running their conventions.[133] The GOP and the Democratic

Party have raised over $200 million in the 2016 cycle so far, and they each report more than $50 million in cash on hand. Why should the people pay for the process of a political party to choose their candidate for the general election? Let the party pay for it. Maybe then they won't need to spend a whopping $20 million for a lavish convention.

We need to reform the way money controls politics and politicians if we hope to restore political power to the people. We can start by simply refusing to financially support any political party. Support the candidate of your choice directly.

Stop volunteering for the military. During my enlistment process I worked with a recruiter to enlist three others and earn an immediate promotion to private first class. After I earned the promotion, I continued to speak at schools and community events, sharing positive and humorous experiences of life in uniform. I now want to add the rest of the story.

In his farewell address, President Eisenhower warned Americans of two new threats facing our country after World War II. The first was our own military-industrial complex. Why warn us about our own military, for which he honorably served in his capacity as a general? I encourage you to read his entire speech for the full context. He viewed the military as a threat to our liberty and our economy.

At that time our military complex required expenditures equal to more than the combined income of all US corporations. Today, military expenditures consume 54 percent of our discretionary spending—nearly $600 billion. We spend about as much per year on our military as the next nine largest military budgets in the world including China, Russia, and the UK. Have you ever asked yourself where all the money goes? Do we really need to spend $600 billion to keep us safe?

President Eisenhower reminded us that "Only an alert and knowledgeable citizenry can compel the proper meshing of the huge industrial and military machinery of defense with our peaceful methods and goals, so that security and liberty may prosper together."[134] We have remained neither alert nor knowledgeable. We traded some of our liberty for promises of security from our government, and we are now risking losing both. The military complex rules our country behind the scenes more than our government tells us. Since Congress does nothing to curtail our military spending, limiting it to what is necessary in these times, we need to take action.

Our military still relies on citizens to volunteer. Our government pays enticing recruiting bonuses, publicly portrays military service as the ultimate patriotic duty (including paying the NFL to allow military participation in pre-game activities),[135] and advertises military service as heroic and honorable. All of these things are true about military service. If that was the only story to tell about our military, we would not have twenty-six veterans committing suicide every day.

I recently watched a Washington Army National Guard (WAARNG) ad shown prior to a movie in a local theatre. It was an amazing ad and made the Guard experience look like the ultimate combination of honor, thrill, patriotism, and valor. I counted all the individual actions in the film, actions where someone in uniform is doing something. The ninety-second ad showed over thirty actions. Of those actions, I performed three in nearly twenty years of service in the WAARNG: pushups, saluting someone, returning a salute—the three most un-remarkable experiences in the ad. Only a minor percentage of Guard soldiers participate in the other experiences, which included rappelling from a helicopter in a storm to rescue someone from a flood.

What does the military do? If we look at a historic timeline of US military action, we see that most of the activities involve small task-force service to protect or evacuate US citizens. I am all for that. Let's keep our special ops groups. What do we need the other 95 percent for? Primarily we use it on treaties and occasional, contrived wars to test new weapons systems. What do we gain by pledging US troops to protect countries that have more than enough oil funds to protect themselves but don't have their own military? We spend our lives and dollars protecting some countries that will not fight for themselves. We receive something in return; at least our government receives some-thing. They tell us we are more secure, but I no longer believe that. I am firmly convinced that the greatest threat to both our security and liberty is our own federal government.

While citizen gun ownership faces scorn in our media, federal agencies now protect themselves against civilian unrest with militarized weapon systems that would make a National Guard combat brigade jealous. These agencies include BLM, DOE, IRS, FDA, EPA, Agriculture, Commerce, Social Security, and the US Postal Service. I have a prediction for people concerned about gun violence by citizens and local police. The federal government is not your savior. It is the biggest threat to your liberty. Give the government more control, as they are currently asking, and you will regret doing so. Our government is moving quickly in a more authoritarian direction. We witnessed in Iraq what an authoritarian democracy is capable of doing to its own citizens. Let's not allow anything resembling that to happen here.

What can we do? I'm glad you asked.

- If you are a suicidal with a story to tell about our military, we need you to tell it. You have a reason to live. You helped protect our country against all enemies, foreign and domestic. We face a domestic threat to our individual liberty. You know about the potential domestic enemy as well as or better than President Eisenhower. Please find a way to share your story. Connect to others you know with similar stories. Stick to the facts, as you know them, and let our fellow Americans come to their own conclusions. This is the way news reporting used to be.

- You can urge your congressman to support bills such as the recently introduced HR 4934; it seeks to demilitarize specific federal agencies. If that bill passes, the enhanced congressional oversight will likely turn up a need for additional curtailment. Inform yourself on the issues and get involved.

- Become an "alert and knowledgeable citizen," as President Eisenhower recommended. I encourage your participation, whether or not you agree with my position. Our democracy needs all of our voices.

Stop volunteering for military service until our government changes the way it uses our military. Let's retain a strong national defense rather than an authoritarian international offense. Our constitution grants the decision to declare war to the House of Representatives, not the president. We ousted a sitting government of another country without a declaration of war and instead used violations of UN provisions to justify our actions. Just as Germany removed certain military powers from its political leader after World War II, we should do the same after Iraq. Our commander-in-chief should not have the authority to authorize this level of military action. A military with no recruits will also force the House and Senate to both renegotiate treaties and curtail the size and scope of the military to what is reasonable and necessary to protect our nation.

Train civilian responders. Attorney Richard Stevens coauthored *Call 911 and Die* in 1999.[136] I read that book about the same time the rural county I lived in adopted the 911 system. The point in the book is not that we should abandon 911; a priority routing of true emergency calls to the proper responders has saved countless lives. The author simply points out that the government and non-government emergency personnel do not have a duty to respond, meaning, in part, we cannot sue them for failing to solve our emergency issues. Some people believe that their first line of defense is to call 911. If the call is properly answered, correctly routed, and the appropriate responders are available, what happens during the time it takes people to arrive? The same is true of other types of emergencies such as school shootings, mall attacks, plane hijackings. A lot of people can die in the time it takes first responders to arrive on the scene.

This section is not an argument for or against gun control. Guns take lives, and save lives. The conversation should be more about increasing training than controlling access.[137] Any weapon, especially guns, in the hands of someone not prepared to use it creates an additional danger for that person and other innocents in the area. This is where some suicidals can help. Many have the training others need to better handle themselves in cases of emergency. Help us help ourselves.

Insurgents fired mortars and rockets against our base in Iraq on nearly a daily basis for several months during our first deployment. As the intel analyst, my responsibilities included briefing the base commander each morning on threat issues. School training alone did not prepare me for duties in active combat. My initial intel briefings consisted of rote, formulaic data. I still clearly remember my briefing the commander stopped by slamming his fists on the table, and yelling, "I know we're going to be hit by mortars today, dammit! I want to know when, where, how many, by whom, and how do we stop them!" They were all great questions to which I had no answer. He didn't fire me; I was the only intel analyst in the unit. I needed to grow into what the situation required.

An early morning attack landed near our command center. A few members of our unit were walking between buildings when they heard the whistle of an incoming mortar. They quickly moved toward cover, but shrapnel cut a main artery of one soldier before he could fully protect himself. If the two others with him had panicked or run indeterminately, cowering and screaming, he would be dead today. Instead, in the midst of additional incoming rounds, they applied appropriate pressure to his wound and carried him to the medic center on our base. Are soldiers trained to react in an emergency this way? Yes. Do all soldiers always respond to all threats with appropriate action? No, not always. Training is one thing; proper emergency action takes mental and emotional practice.

The number of times mortars and rockets landed just off target or landed on a target, where lives could have been lost had the explosive detonated, seemed nothing short of a miracle in the proportions experienced by George Washington during the revolutionary war. Do prayer and faith mean nothing bad will happen, or no one will die in combat? Absolutely not. Does it make a difference? Definitely.[138]

Quick thinking and properly trained people save lives. In 2015 a civilian probably saved the lives of several people when he killed a gunman inside a West Philadelphia barbershop,[139] and an Uber driver wounded a gunman who opened fire on a crowd of people in Chicago.[140]

When an emergency happens, such as a school or mall shooting, if professional responders are not already on the scene, there is a gap in time that either the perpetrator or the people will own. If people panic, run screaming in no particular direction, criminals own that time. If enough civilians are trained to respond appropriately, we the people own that time.

I worked with a taskforce after 9/11 to create a response plan for the state of Washington. We discussed the concept of armed civilians, and most of the people around the table did not want civilians engaging with perpetrators. Civilian engagement makes the professional responders' jobs more difficult and more dangerous. We can incorporate civilians into a national response program without increasing difficulty or risk factors for professionals. Fortunately, government discussions now lean in that direction as well.

The tragic November 2015 terrorist attack in Paris demonstrated a compelling case for training civilians; police arrived on the scene 140 minutes after the shooting started, and emergency medical personnel, by protocol, reached victims only after police cleared the threat. Clearing the threat added an additional twenty minutes before victims received aid.[141] People died before medical personnel reached them. Civilians who know proper ways to respond in various emergencies will save lives.

Whether or not the US government ever starts an official civilian training program, here are some steps you can take to help ensure greater homeland security:

- Follow all the rules for concealed carries.
- Professional responders, including the police, are on our side. Everyone wants to go home safe. Do not pose a threat to responders when they arrive.

- Follow appropriate weapon safety. If your weapon of choice is a gun, for example, never point a gun at someone unless you intend to shoot that person.
- Know your target and what is beyond or around your target. No one wants friendly fire, unintended causalities, or collateral damage. You can be liable.
- Become certified in emergency first aid.
- Take the Department of Defense's Terrorism Awareness course.[142]
- Read, study, and practice the tips in Homeland Security's guide on how to respond in an active shooter scenario.[143]
- If you are engaging when responders arrive, expect to be hand-cuffed or detained. You look like a bad guy to them in that moment. Cooperate, and you will be okay. In my one episode with a weapon when officers arrived on a scene, I placed the weapon on the ground with the chamber visibly empty. I held my hands in the air, palms open, facing them. I answered questions calmly, not talking over them or shouting at them. They appreciated my cooperation immensely as they handcuffed me while checking my story.
- Know how to relay accurate information about who, what, where, and when. This is not a time for speculation or exaggeration.
- Do not panic. Help others remain calm.

Suicidals, we need you. You were willing to kill yourselves perhaps because you viewed yourselves as bad. I have not yet met a suicidal I would call a "bad person," including myself, even though I labeled myself such for years. Can you redirect your actions against those who truly threaten our society? I don't want you to have access to any weapons while you potentially pose a danger to yourself or others. Even without a weapon you can be trained in proper response techniques, train others, and advocate for civilian emergency response legislation.

Let's work on you getting back to being the person who wanted to be part of a rewarding and life-saving mission.

Volunteer with suicidals. The most important action any suicidal can take to move beyond his or her suicidal ideology, build stronger communities, and potentially impact a national agenda is to volunteer to work with other suicidals. You might not be ready today. That's okay. Get started regardless. At least you will find out what you need to do to become qualified. Ask for help getting there. Meet other suicidals who volunteer, and listen to their stories.

The need is huge these days. Crisis centers around the country rely on volunteers to staff phone lines or online chats. If you are a veteran, check out opportunities at your nearest VA. I recommend that you start with people who are a lot like you: a troubled teen, someone in the homeless community, a veteran, a busy professional, or an anxious financial banker. How can you reach someone with your story?

I thought about this book for almost a year before I started writing. I did not want to share my story. I did not want to become a suicide awareness poster boy. What changed? I began volunteering. I shared my story with individuals. Then, realizing that I do not have the time or energy to reach as many people as I want if I stick to one-on-one conversations, I wrote this book as a way of sharing because I care. I care, in part, because others cared about me.

In case there is someone who, after reading this book, still believes right now that no one cares for you, I want you to hear me. I care. If you were here, you could see it in my eyes. I could introduce you to dozens, if not hundreds, of people I know who also care about you. Maybe you have a voice in your head like I did that says, "That's easy to say when you don't know me." You're right. However, they know me, and they still care. I have not been the easiest person to care about. I've emotionally pushed people away, hurt people, and ostracized myself. Yet there they are, caring for and loving me all the same. It's crazy, right? The only thing they ask of me is to do the same for others.

Volunteering works more like paying it forward than paying it back. Let go of any thought that you need to earn someone caring for you. You can't repay caring. It doesn't work that way. Appreciate people who care for you. However, forcing something on them that you think will mean as much to them as what they did for you insults people. Accept the gift. Say thank you. Do you want to do something about it to return the favor? Do the same for others. Be there for someone else in the same way.

I challenge you and *dare* you to look for an opportunity to serve right now. The life you save just might be your own.

Crisis Planning

Signs that I am in crisis:

★

★

★

★

People I trust to help me in crisis:

Name: _____ Email: _____ Phone: _____
What I want this person to do:

Name: _____ Email: _____ Phone: _____
What I want this person to do:

Medications that help me:

Mental health or medical providers:

Name: _____ Email: _____ Phone: _____
Name: _____ Email: _____ Phone: _____
Name: _____ Email: _____ Phone: _____

Activities that help me:

Please do not:

How to tell when I am no longer in crisis:

Endnotes

[1] A portion of a suicide note by Daniel Somers. I encourage you to read the entire note. "The Suicide Note of Daniel Somers," *The Washington Times*. http://twt-media.washtimes.com/media/community/misc/2013/06/27/the-suicide-of-daniel-somers-note.pdf.

[2] I use the term *suicidal* as a noun to describe anyone who contemplates suicide as a real solution to his or her problems.

[3] For an excellent philosophical discussion of whether or not we owe a duty to God, others, or ourselves to stay alive, see David Hume, *On Suicide*, (1796).

[4] For most of my life, I believed selfishness was a sin, as if every decision I made needed to consider the effects on others more than the effects on my own life. This belief led to some of the most disastrous decisions of my life. I later learned that I am expected to make my own decisions and live my own life. I learned that self-determination is a virtue. This duality of selfishness versus self-determination undermines a healthy psyche for individuals and their communities. God's steering does nothing for a parked car.

[5] http://www.kurtcobainssuicidenote.com/kurt_cobains_suicide_note.html.

[6] Samuel Butler, *Hudibras*. Part III, Canto iii, lines 547–550.

[7] Sam Frizell, "9 Musicians Remember Kurt Cobain," *TIME*, April 5, 2014. http://time.com/50739/kurt-cobain-anniversary-nirvana/.

[8] Edgar Dahl, "Im Schatten des Hippokrates / Assistierter Suizid und ärztliches Ethos müssen sich nicht widersprechen." *Humanes Leben – Humanes Sterben*, 4/2008, 66–67, quoted in "Principles / Philosophy," Digitas. http://

dignitas.ch/index.php?option=com content&view=article&id=10&lang=
en&Itemid=0.

9   Linda Thompson, "The Clinton Body Count: Coincidence or The Kiss
    of Death," *First Principles Archive.* https://www.fpparchive.org/media/
    documents/war on terrorism/The%20Clinton%20Body%20Count;%
    20Coincidence%20or%20the%20Kiss%20of%20Death Linda%20D.%
    20Thompson 1993 AEN%20News.pdf.

10 Martin Gould and Alana Goodman, "Outrage at Julian Assange for impli-
    cating murdered DNC staffer in email leak and offering $20k reward - as
    the victim's parents accuse Wikileaks founder of 'politicizing this horrible
    tragedy'," *Daily Mail,* August 10, 2016. http://www.dailymail.co.uk/news/
    article-3726250/Enemies-Hillary-Bill-say-27-year-old-murder-victim-Seth-
    Rich-suspected-leaking-DNC-emails-belongs-Clinton-Death-List-people-
    ties-couple-died-time.html#ixzz4H1iKctiF

11 *Stars and Stripes* maintains a Special Report page on military suicide sto-
    ries and links about suicide issues at http://www.stripes.com/news/
    special-reports/suicide-in-the-military.

12 The Washington Death with Dignity Act (2009), Revised Code of Washington,
    Chapter 70, Section 245.

13 CA Leardmann, TM Powell, TC Smith, et al, "Risk Factors Associated With
    Suicide in Current and Former US Military Personnel," *JAMA,* August 7,
    2013, Vol 310, No. 5, 496–506. http://jama.jamanetwork.com/article.aspx?
    articleid=1724276.

14 Militaries blow things up and kill people. Sure, we can send them on a
    humanitarian mission every so often to help everyone feel better about
    themselves. A recent recruiting ad for the Washington Army National Guard
    featured uniformed personnel performing heroic, life-saving missions. I
    counted thirty-nine different actions in that ad. Of those thirty-nine, I per-
    formed three in my nineteen years in the Guard. I saluted, have been saluted,
    and participated in PT drills. I know very few guardsmen who ever get to do
    any of the heroic actions portrayed in that ad. Is it misleading? We motivate
    people to sign up with this portrayal of service and then, too often, the new
    service members find out their first mission has them playing the role of an
    expendable pawn in an international chess game.

[15] "I Survived My Suicide Attempt," ExperienceProject. http://www.experienceproject.com/stories/Survived-My-Suicide-Attempt/3469103

[16] Father William Byron, "Do people who commit suicide go to hell?" *Catholic Digest*, April 01, 2007. http://www.catholicdigest.com/articles/faith/knowledge/2007/04-01/do-people-who-commit-suicide-go-to-hell. I encourage people interested in the discussion of suicide and hell to investigate the teachings of different denominations and religions.

[17] Alice Turner, *The History of Hell*, (Orlando: Hardcourt, Brace and Co., 1993).

[18] "Thomas Aquinas, Saint," *Catholic Encyclopedia*. http://www.catholic.com/encyclopedia/thomas-aquinas-saint.

[19] Luke 13:1-5. "Now on the same occasion there were some present who reported to Him about the Galileans whose blood Pilate had mixed with their sacrifices. ² And Jesus said to them, 'Do you suppose that these Galileans were greater sinners than all other Galileans because they suffered this fate? ³ I tell you, no, but unless you repent, you will all likewise perish. ⁴ Or do you suppose that those eighteen on whom the tower in Siloam fell and killed them were worse culprits than all the men who live in Jerusalem? ⁵ I tell you, no, but unless you repent, you will all likewise perish.'"

[20] For one survey of various statistics see http://lostallhope.com/suicide-statistics. You will be asked to confirm that you are at least eighteen years of age to read this article.

[21] For some stories about unsuccessful suicides see http://www.suicide.org/attempted-suicide-horrors.html.

[22] Sara Fritz, "Daniel, 1988-2000: A child's suicide, unending grief and lessons learned," *The St. Petersburg Times*, November 16, 2003. http://www.sptimes.com/2003/11/16/Floridian/Daniel_1988_2000_A_.shtml.

[23] Although the VA's Cognitive Processing Therapy procedure is a not a Twelve-Step program, there are similarities. Both begin with a desire to stop living out a pattern of suicidal behavior. Confronting harm to others begins in step four. For more information on Suicide Anonymous or to download a free copy of their book see http://www.suicideanonymous.net/Home_Page.html.

24   Ethics are the moral principles that govern a person's or group's behavior. While some may argue that ethical suicide is an oxymoron, I argue that ethics around suicide already exist. Stating that suicide is always wrong is both incorrect and not an ethical position.

25   "If your enemy is hungry, give him food to eat; And if he is thirsty, give him water to drink; For you will heap burning coals on his head, And the Lord will reward you." Proverbs 25:21–22.

Solomon's proverbs are not spiritual absolutes, but are his observations about life in his time. I find his sayings accurately reflect our day as well. Humans have not changed much in the three thousand years since Solomon's reign over Israel.

26   "Survivor Stories," ChildSuicide. http://www.childsuicide.org/survivorstories.html.

27   Sara Swan Miller, *An Empty Chair: Living in The Wake of a Sibling's Suicide*, (iUniverse, Inc., 2000). Interviews with more than thirty sibling survivors all over the US, as well as the author's own account of losing a sister to suicide.

Alison Wertheimer, *A Special Scar: The Experience of People Bereaved by Suicide*, (New York: Routledge Publications, 2001). The author, who lost her sister to suicide, presents interviews with fifty survivors, covering a wide range of issues, including the press, stigma, guilt, anger, and rejection.

28   Gregg Zoroya, "40,000 Suicides Annually, Yet America Simply Shrugs," *USA Today,* October 09, 2014. http://www.usatoday.com/longform/news/nation/2014/10/09/suicide-mental-health-prevention-research/15276353/.

29   Kimberly A. Van Orden, et. al., "The Interpersonal Theory of Suicide," *Psychological Review,* April 2010, vol. 117(2), 575–600. http://dx.doi.org/10.1037/a0018697.

30   Tracking the source and explanation of this cost estimate was the most frustrating part of my research. Given that this number is so widely circulated, I am stunned at the general acceptance in the media of the assumptions behind the calculation method. If the reader is interested in discovering how this number is calculated, I suggest beginning with the Centers for Disease Control's "Cost of Injury Report Help Menu" available online at http://www.cdc.gov/injury/wisqars/cost_help/estimation_framework.html.

31   Although 198 is the number frequently quoted as the number of nationalities in the United States, this number is not easy to track or define. For example, see Susan Saulny, "Counting by Race Can Throw Off Some Numbers," *NY Times*, February 9, 2011.

32   Perhaps a representation of the major occupational groups as listed in the US Department of Labor, Bureau of Labor Statistics, *Occupational Outlook Handbook*. http://www.bls.gov/ooh/.

33   Interactive Graph, "Top 10 Causes of Death in the United States, 1900–2010," *New England Journal of Medicine*. http://www.nejm.org/action/show-MediaPlayer?doi=10.1056%2FNEJMp1113569&aid=NEJMp1113569 attach 1&area=&.

34   James C. Scott, *Seeing Like a State*, (New Haven: Yale University Press, 1998). Although suicide is not one of the discussion points in Scott's book, his description of when a state entity's views leads to its failure to improve social conditions, applies to suicide as well. The United States' definition of the suicide problem is part of the problem.

35   John Stellars, *Stoicism*, (Berkeley: University of California Press, 2006).

36   Joan Blades and Matt Kibbe, "Are Police Stealing People's Property?" *The Daily Beast*, January 2, 2015.

37   Acts 7:56. "and he said, 'Behold, I see the heavens opened up and the Son of Man standing at the right hand of God.'"

38   Revelation 20:4. "Then I saw thrones, and they sat on them, and judgment was given to them. And I saw the souls of those who had been beheaded because of their testimony of Jesus and because of the word of God, and those who had not worshiped the beast or his image, and had not received the mark on their forehead and on their hand; and they came to life and reigned with Christ for a thousand years."

39   1 Peter 4:14, 16.

40   Matthew 5:11.

41   George Howe Colt, *November of the Soul: The Enigma of Suicide*, (New York: Simon and Schuster, 2006), 152–155.

[42] Bishop Charles Joseph Hefele, *A History of the Councils of the Church: From the Original Documents* (Edinburgh: T. & T. Clark, 1896), vol. 5.

[43] Alexander Murray, *Suicide in the Middle Ages: vol. 2: The Curse on Self-Murder*, (Oxford: Oxford University Press, 2000).

[44] William Hazlitt, *The Table Talk of Martin Luther*, (London: H.G. Bohn, 1857), 589.

[45] Ibid., 738.

[46] James N. Butcher, Susan Mineka, and Jill M. Hooley, *Abnormal Psychology* (Boston: Pearson Education, Inc., 16th ed., 2013). Most of the early time line is based on this work.

[47] Paul Jay Fink and Allan Tasman, *Stigma and Mental Illness* (Washington, D.C.: American Psychiatric Press, Inc., 1992).

[48] Dorothea Dix, *Memorial to the Legislature of Massachusetts, 1843* (Boston: Directors of The Old South Work, 1904). https://archive.org/details/memorialtolegisl00dixd.

[49] Edgar Allan Poe, "The System of Doctor Tarr and Professor Fether," *Graham Magazine*, November, 1845. http://poestories.com/read/systemoftarr. I am also a fan of the Alan Parson's Project song of the same title.

[50] Elizabeth Jane Cochrane, *Ten Days In a Madhouse* (New York: Ian L. Munro, 1887). http://digital.library.upenn.edu/women/bly/madhouse/madhouse.html.

[51] J. H. Kellogg, *Plain Facts for Old and Young* (Iowa: Segner & Condit, 1881), 453. http://www.gutenberg.org/files/19924/19924-h/19924-h.htm#p478.

[52] Clifford Whittingham Beers, *A Mind that Found Itself* (New York: Longman, Green and Co., 1913). http://www.gutenberg.org/files/11962/11962-h/11962-h.htm.

[53] For good discussions of the background issues leading to this legislation in the US, see Gerald N. Grob, *From Asylum to Community: Mental Health Policy in Modern America* (Princeton: Princeton University Press, 1991), chapter 3. For a similar discussion of issues in the UK, see Ian Shaw and Hugh Middleton *Understanding Treatment Without Consent: An Analysis of the Work of the Mental Health Act Commission* (Farnham: Ashgate Publishing, Ltd., 2008), chapter 1.

[54] Thomas S. Szasz, "The Myth of Mental Illness," *American Psychologist*, 15, 113–118. http://psychclassics.yorku.ca/Szasz/myth.htm.

[55] For another view of the impact of Szasz's work see Jeffrey Oliver, "The Myth of Thomas Szasz," The New Atlantis, Number 13, Summer 2006, 68–84. http://www.thenewatlantis.com/publications/the-myth-of-thomas-szasz.

[56] Erving Goffman, *Asylums: Essays on the Social Situation of Mental Patients and Other Inmates* (New York: Anchor Books, 1961).

[57] Dr. Raymond M. Weinstein, "Goffman's Asylums and the Social Situation of Mental Patients," *Orthomolecular Psychiatry*, vol. 11, no. 4, 1982, 267–274. http://orthomolecular.org/library/jom/1982/pdf/1982-v11n04-p267.pdf.

[58] Richard D. Lyons, "How Release Of Mental Patients Began," NY Times, October 30, 1984. http://www.nytimes.com/1984/10/30/science/how-release-of-mental-patients-began.html?pagewanted=1

Alexandar Thomas, "Ronald Reagan and the Commitment of the Mentally Ill: Capital, Interest Groups, and the Eclipse of Social Policy," *Electronic Journal of Sociology*, Vol. 3, No. 4, 1998. http://sociology.org/content/vol003.004/thomas_d.html

[59] U.S. Public Health Service, "The Surgeon General's Call to Action to Prevent Suicide," Washington, DC, 1999. http://profiles.nlm.nih.gov/ps/access/nnbbbh.pdf

[60] For additional reading see:

A. M. Foerschner, "The History of Mental Illness: From 'Skull Drills' to 'Happy Pills'," Inquiries Journal, Vol. 2, No. 9, 2010. http://www.inquiriesjournal.com/articles/283/the-history-of-mental-illness-from-skull-drills-to-happy-pills.

National Institutes of Health, "Important Events In NIMH History." http://www.nih.gov/about/almanac/organization/NIMH.htm#events.

[61] James Allen, *As a Man Thinketh* (UK: The Savoy Publishing Co., 1903). Available at http://www.gutenberg.org/files/4507/4507-h/4507-h.htm.

[62] Frank Selden, *Power Talk*, Video, Center for Spiritual Living, Seattle, filmed Feb 2, 2014. http://youtu.be/tjfb8k4g3Wk?list=PLWilu0kYmiP5ZanvNaqAFhWGslzaMTi6H.

63 Martin Luther King, *Strength To Love* (Minneapolis: Fortress Press, 2010), 131.

64 Brian L. Mishara, "Reconciling Clinical Experience with Evidence-Based Knowledge in Suicide Prevention Policy and Practice," *Crisis* 2008; Vol. 29(1):1–3.

65 Anonymous, "Why I Don't Cry to Christians Anymore," Posted by Micah J. Murrah on Feb. 5, 2015 at http://micahjmurray.com/why-i-dont-cry-to-christians/.

66 "Suicide Prevention," US Department of Veterans Affairs. http://www.mentalhealth.va.gov/suicide_prevention/index.asp

67 https://contextualscience.org.

68 http://www.abct.org/Home/.

69 http://behavioraltech.org/resources/crd.cfm. Terms must be accepted to use this directory.

70 John Locke, "Essay Concerning Human Understanding," Ed. Kenneth Winkler (Indianapolis: Hackett Publishing, 1996), 33.

71 Before using the list on the top of the next page, try closing your eyes and thinking about what is most important to you about how you show up in the world. What about YOU brings you happiness? You will probably find that you already possess all these traits to some degree. Which ones do you want to enhance to magnify the life you want to live?

Accountable	Candid	Creative	Energetic
Adaptable	Capable	Curious	Enthusiastic
Adventurous	Charismatic	Dedicated	Ethical
Alert	Clear	Determine	Excited
Ambitious	Collaborative	Diplomatic	Expressive
Appropriate	Committed	Direct	Fair
Assertive	Compassion	Disciplined	Faithful
Astute	Connected	Dynamic	Fearless
Attentive	Conscious	Easygoing	Flexible
Authentic	Considerate	Effective	Friendly
Aware	Consistent	Efficient	Generative
Brave	Cooperative	Empathetic	Generous
Calm	Courageous	Empowering	Grateful

Happy	Joyful	Playful	Spiritual
Honest	Knowing	Poised	Spontaneous
Honorable	Leading	Polite	Stable
Humorous	Listener	Powerful	Strong
Imaginative	Lively	Practical	Successful
Immaculate	Logical	Proactive	Supportive
Independent	Loving	Productive	Tactful
Industrious	Loyal	Reliable	Trusting
Innovative	Networker	Resourceful	Trustworthy
Inquiring	Nurturing	Responsible	Truthful
Integrity	Open-Minded	Self-confident	Versatile
Intelligent	Optimistic	Self-reliant	Vibrant
Intentional	Organized	Sensual	Warm
Interesting	Patient	Sincere	Willing
Intimate	Peaceful	Skillful	Wise
			Zealous

72 For Benjamin Franklin's method, including how he defined his own terms, I recommend reading his entire autobiography. Go to a used book store and pick one up for about three dollars. It will help you change your life more than spending that three dollars on a latte. Read it, mark it up, and read it again. To get started specifically at the section on his method of daily evaluation see: http://www.ushistory.org/franklin/autobiography/page38.htm.

73 Dalai Lama XIV Bstan-'dzin-rgya-mtsho, Kloñ-chen-pa Dri-med-'od-zer, *Mind in Comfort and Ease: The Vision of Enlightenment in the Great Perfection* (Somerville, MA: Wisdom Publications, 2007), 124.

74 Dr. Maxwell Maltz, *Psycho-Cynernetics* (New York: Simon & Shuster, 1969).

75 "The Essentials for Traveling in Bear Country," Alaska Department of Natural Resources. http://dnr.alaska.gov/parks/units/kodiak/kodbears.htm.

76 David J Morris, "The VA Treated My PTSD All Wrong," *The Washington Post*, November 22, 2015. https://www.washingtonpost.com/posteverything/wp/2015/11/11/the-va-treated-my-ptsd-all-wrong/.

77 For more information about MKP's New Warrior Training Adventure, see http://mankindproject.org/new-warrior-training-adventure.

78 For more information about Vet's Journey Home see http://www.vets journeyhome.org/.

79 William Danforth, *I Dare You* (St. Louis: American Youth Foundation, 1985). Danforth discusses the four-fold foundation of physical, mental, social, religious. Originally published in 1931, this book is a true classic and one of my favorites. Don't merely read it, practice the exercises. I dare you to live it!

80 James J. Mazza, et al., "An Examination of the Validity of Retrospective Measures of Suicide Attempts in Youth," *Journal of Adolescent Health*, Volume 49, Issue 5, 532–537.

81 Theodor Suess Geisel, *Oh, The Places You'll Go!* (New York, NY: Random House, 1990).

82 Leo. F. Buscaglia, *Love: What Life is All About* (New York, NY: Ballantine Books, 1996), 26.

83 Henry Brean, "Suicide at M Resort blamed on loss of free buffet for life," *Las Vegas Review-Journal* April 6, 2015. http://www.reviewjournal.com/news/ las-vegas/suicide-m-resort-blamed-loss-free-buffet-life.

84 One could be tempted to add "Who would even think of such a ghastly concept?" I would. It's how my brain works. I sometimes wonder whether I should write fiction, but, so far, my fiction is too real for people and makes them question the safety they see in their lives. It's perhaps better to temporarily scare people with large rabid dogs or demonic cars that don't exist. Plus, I think I suck at writing fiction. How do I deal with my constant barrage of fear-inducing mental images? Simple. I'm not afraid to die.

85 Another fallacious argument is "affirming the consequent." The antecedent in an indicative conditional is claimed to be true because the consequent is true; if A, then B; B, therefore A. I taught LSAT (the exam used in law school admissions) prep for Kaplan during law school and found this to be the most common error made by students on the logic section of the test. The doctor's fallacy is more complicated than this because she introduces a third factor. If suicide, then disorder. If disorder, then treatable. If treatable, then no suicide. I strongly disagree with both consequents.

86 Dr. Peg Sandeen, "Brittany Maynard and the Right to Die with Dignity," MSNBC, November 14, 2104. http://www.msnbc.com/msnbc/brittany- maynard-and-the-right-die-dignity.

87   "Peer Support Groups," U.S. Department of Veterans Affairs. http://www.ptsd.va.gov/public/treatment/cope/peer_support_groups.asp.

88   Julie Bosman, "Pine Ridge Indian Reservation Struggles With Suicides Among Its Young," *NY Times* May 01, 2015. http://www.nytimes.com/2015/05/02/us/pine-ridge-indian-reservation-struggles-with-suicides-among-young-people.html?_r=0.

89   Onora O'Neill, "What we don't understand about trust," TEDxHousesOfParliament, Filmed Jun 2013. https://www.ted.com/talks/onora_o_neill_what_we_don_t_understand_about_trust?language=en.

90   In that vehicle style the turret gunner sat in a strip or sling about nine-to-ten wide. One end of the sling was securely fastened to the vehicle. A hook on the other end fit into a quick release lever that could be activated from the inside in case of emergency. Flipping that lever when the gunner was not otherwise braced to drop inside could cause some bumps and bruises but nothing like a shrapnel blast.

91   "Suicide Hotlines," Suicide.Org. http://www.suicide.org/suicide-hotlines.html.

92   "Suicide Data," World Health Organization. http://www.who.int/mental_health/prevention/suicide/suicideprevent/en/.

93   "King County Mental Health Services," King County. http://www.kingcounty.gov/healthservices/MentalHealth/Services/CrisisServices/CommitmentServices.aspx.

94   "Criteria for a Major Depressive Episode," BipolarLab. http://www.bipolar-lab.com/index.php?option=com_content&view=article&id=49:mdecriteria&catid=21:bipolar&Itemid=77.

95   "Module 4 – Suicide Risk Assessment," Suicide Prevention Resource Center. http://www.sprc.org/sites/sprc.org/files/PrimerModule4.pdf.

96   Bob Nicas, "A Date With Death on the Golden Gate Bridge," Vice Communications, August 7, 2012. http://www.vice.com/read/komp-laint-dept-a-date-with-death-on-the-golden-gate-bridge.

97   For example, this open opportunity posting from the Arkansas Crisis Center: https://www.givepulse.com/event/12142-Save-A-Life-by-Listening!

98 "2012 National Strategy for Suicide Prevention: Goals and Objectives for Action," U.S. Department of Health and Human Services Office of the Surgeon General and National Action Alliance for Suicide Prevention, Washington, DC, September 2012. Objective 5.1. This publication may be downloaded or ordered at www.surgeongeneral.gov/library/reports/national-strategy-suicide-prevention/index.html.

99 JAC Rietjens, et. Al., "Two Decades of Research on Euthanasia from the Netherlands. What Have We Learnt and What Questions Remain?" *Journal of Bioethical Inquiry*, 2009, Vol. 6, No. 3, 271–283. http://www.ncbi.nlm.nih.gov/pmc/articles/PMC2733179/.

100 "National strategy for suicide prevention: Goals and objectives for action," U.S. Dept. of Health and Human Services, 2001. http://www.sprc.org/sites/sprc.org/files/library/nssp.pdf.

101 "2012 National Strategy for Suicide Prevention: Goals and Objectives for Action," pg. 11. http://www.surgeongeneral.gov/library/reports/national-strategy-suicide-prevention/index.html.

102 John 15:13.

103 John 10:11.

104 John 8: 10–11. "Straightening up, Jesus said to her, 'Woman, where are they? Did no one condemn you?' 11 She said, 'No one, Lord.' And Jesus said, 'I do not condemn you, either. Go. From now on sin no more.'"

105 Linkin Park, *Leave Out All the Rest*, Album, Warner Bros. Records, 100731-2, 2007.

106 Kurt M. Hartman and Bryan A. Liang, "Exceptions to Informed Consent in Emergency Medicine," *Hospital Physician*, March 1999, 53–59. http://www.turner-white.com/pdf/hp_mar99_emergmed.pdf.

107 Revised Code of Washington, Title 71, Chapter 32, Section 260. http://apps.leg.wa.gov/rcw/default.aspx?cite=71.32.260.

108 Yoichiro Takayanagi, Adam P. Spira, et. al., "Antidepressant Use and Lifetime History of Mental Disorders in a Community Sample: Results from the Baltimore Epidemiologic Catchment Area Study," *Journal of Clinical Psychiatry*, 2015, Vol. 76, No. 1, 40–44.

[109] "What are the Real Risks of Antidepressants?" Harvard Health Publications, May 2005. http://www.health.harvard.edu/mind-and-mood/what_are_the_real_risks_of_antidepressants.

[110] Li Hui, Xiao-Jing Guo, Xiao-Fei Ye, et al., "Adverse Drug Reactions of Spontaneous Reports in Shanghai Pediatric Population," *PLoS ONE*, 2014, Vol. 9, No. 2. http://journals.plos.org/plosone/article?id=10.1371/journal.pone.0089829.

[111] John M. Kane, Delbert G. Robinson, Nina R. Schooler, et. al., "Comprehensive Versus Usual Community Care for First-Episode Psychosis: 2-Year Outcomes from the NIMH RAISE Early Treatment Program," *American Journal of Psychiatry*, Volume 173, Issue 4, April 01, 2016, pp. 362-372. http://dx.doi.org/10.1176/appi.ajp.2015.15050632

[112] Daryn Kagan, *One Stupid Thing To Stop Saying About Cancer*, Blog post, January 18, 2015. https://darynkagan.wordpress.com/2015/01/18/one-stupid-thing-to-stop-saying-about-cancer/.

[113] Ed Cumming, "Should we do anything we can to keep people alive?" *The Guardian*, October 25, 2014. http://www.theguardian.com/lifeandstyle/2014/oct/26/should-we-do-anything-we-can-to-keep-people-alive#comments.

[114] Atul Gawande, *Being Mortal: Medicine and What Matters in the End* (New York: Metropolitan Books, 2014), 171–172.

[115] Danielle Ofri, "The Tyranny of Perfection," *Slate Magazine*, September, 2014. http://www.slate.com/articles/health_and_science/medical_examiner/2014/09/suicide_in_medical_doctors_physicians_suffer_from_stress_self_doubt_fear.html.

[116] Pauline Anderson, "Physician Health Programs: More Harm Than Good?" Medscape, August 19, 2015. http://www.medscape.com/viewarticle/849772. Medscape login required (free registration).

[117] Deborah Brauser, "Complaint Process Linked to Depression, Suicidal Thoughts in Docs," Medscape, January 16, 2015. http://www.medscape.com/viewarticle/838286. Medscape login required (free registration).

[118] Hermione Elliott, "Striking a Chord," Living Well, Dying Well. http://www.lwdwtraining.uk/about-livingwell-dyingwell/striking-a-chord/.

[119] Sebastian Junger, "Our lonely society makes it hard to come home from war," TED Talks Live, Filmed Nov 2015. https://www.ted.com/talks/sebastian_junger_our_lonely_society_makes_it_hard_to_come_home_from_war?language=en.

[120] Amanda Holpuch, "US death rate rose for the first time in a decade in 2015," *The Guardian*, June 1, 2016. http://www.theguardian.com/us-news/2016/jun/01/us-death-rate-rose-first-time-decade-2015.

[121] Newsboys, *Wherever We Go*, Album, Inpop Records, 1383, 2006.

[122] Doctors Without Borders. http://www.doctorswithoutborders.org/.

[123] Up With People. http://www.upwithpeople.org/.

[124] Seattle's Union Gospel Mission. http://www.ugm.org/.

[125] "What your baby looks like: 12 weeks," BabyCenter. http://www.babycenter.com/fetal-development-images-12-weeks

[126] Natalie Staats Reiss and Mark Dombeck, "Suicide Statistics," MentalHelp. https://www.mentalhelp.net/articles/suicide-statistics/

[127] "Homelessness: A silent killer," Crisis. http://www.crisis.org.uk/data/files/publications/Homelessness%20-%20a%20silent%20killer.pdf.

[128] "Debt Limit - A Guide To American Federal Debt Made Easy," Video, YouTube. https://www.youtube.com/watch?v=Li0no7O9zmE.

[129] "Suicide," King County. http://www.kingcounty.gov/healthservices/health/data/GunViolence/suicide.aspx.

[130] To read what Utah did to end chronic homelessness see their excellent "Comprehensive Report On Homelessness." https://jobs.utah.gov/housing/scso/documents/homelessness2014.pdf.

[131] J. Dana Stuster, "Mapped: The 7 Governments the U.S. Has Overthrown," *Foreign Policy*, August 20, 2013. http://foreignpolicy.com/2013/08/20/mapped-the-7-governments-the-u-s-has-overthrown/.

[132] Richard Baehr, "The Sound of Stealing," *The American Thinker*, Dec. 17, 2004. http://www.americanthinker.com/articles/2004/12/the_sound_of_stealing.html.

133 Stephen Dinan, "Struggling DNC craves tax dollars for convention," *The Washington Times*, December 13, 2015. http://www.washingtontimes.com/news/2015/dec/13/dnc-craves-tax-dollars-for-convention/?page=all.

134 "Transcript of President Dwight D. Eisenhower's Farewell Address (1961)," OurDocuments. https://www.ourdocuments.gov/doc.php?doc=90&page=transcript.

135 Eben Novy-Williams, "NFL to Pay Back Money Collected for Military Tributes," *Bloomberg*, November 4, 2015. http://www.bloomberg.com/news/articles/2015-11-04/nfl-to-refund-taxpayer-money-paid-to-teams-for-military-tributes.

136 Richard W. Stevens, *Dial 911 and Die*, (Hartford, WI: Mazel Freedom Press, 1999).

137 For two excellent books on the subject see: John Lott, Jr., *More Guns, Less Crime*, (Chicago: University of Chicago Press, 2010). 3rd ed.

Richard Poe, *The Seven Myths of Gun Control: Reclaiming the truth about guns, crime, and the Second Amendment*, (Roseville, CA: Prima Publishing, 2001).

138 Frank Selden, *Finding Faith in the Fury*, (Sisters, OR: VMI Publishers, 2006).

139 David Chang, "Gunman Shot, Killed Inside West Philly Barbershop," *NBC Philadelphia*, March 22, 2015. http://www.nbcphiladelphia.com/news/local/Man-Shot-in-the-Chest-Inside-West-Philly-Barbershop-297176271.html.

140 Geoff Ziezulewicz, "Uber driver, licensed to carry gun, shoots gunman in Logan Square." *Chicago Tribune*, April 20, 2015. http://www.chicagotribune.com/news/local/breaking/ct-uber-driver-shoots-gunman-met-0420-20150419-story.html.

141 Heather Horn, "Fighting Terrorism With Tourniquets," *The Atlantic*, Nov 20, 2015. http://www.theatlantic.com/international/archive/2015/11/first-aid-emergency-response-terrorism/417054/.

142 "Level I Antiterrorism Awareness Training," Joint Knowledge Online. http://jko.jten.mil/courses/atl1/launch.html.

143 "Active Shooter, How to Respond," United States Department of Homeland Security. https://www.dhs.gov/xlibrary/assets/active_shooter_booklet.pdf.